LANCASHIRE'S
HISTORIC
PUBS

PETER THOMAS

SUTTON PUBLISHING

Sutton Publishing Limited
Phoenix Mill · Thrupp · Stroud
Gloucestershire · GL5 2BU

First published 2006

Copyright © Peter Thomas, 2006

Title page photograph: One of the tenth-
century Celtic crosses at Whalley
(see p. 92).

British Library Cataloguing in Publication Data
A catalogue record for this book is available from the
British Library.

ISBN 0-7509-4219-3

Typeset in 10.5/13.5 Photina.
Typesetting and origination by
Sutton Publishing Limited.
Printed and bound in England by
J.H. Haynes & Co. Ltd, Sparkford.

A short distance from the Redwell Inn at Arkholme is the delightful river walk along the Lune at Kirkby Lonsdale.

CONTENTS

The exterior of the Old Man & Scythe at Bolton (see pp. 30–3).

The packhorse bridge and church at Croston (see pp. 52–5).

INTRODUCTION

The pub is so much part of our tradition that, like the village green or the marketplace, it seems to have been with us throughout our history. Yet it was not always as it is now, neither was it originally called a public house; today's 'local', however small, is licensed and regulated, a far cry from the early drinking houses where home-brewed ale was sold.

Scraps of evidence tell us that barley was being grown in England long before the Romans came; their writers suggest that an intoxicating drink was already being produced here through the soaking of grain. How much earlier is difficult to say, but one can imagine that the knowledge of how to brew and the attractive product would have been eagerly passed on. This would, of course, have been a domestic brew consumed at home; perhaps if there was a surplus it was bartered or sold.

The Roman *tabernae*, or drinking places, in their settlements and along the many miles of Roman roads, mark the first use of the word 'tavern' that we can recognise in our day. The Romans distinguished these premises with a bunch of vine leaves outside; wine was the most common drink, although ale was sold as well. Apart from this, we have the voice of the Christian Church condemning drunkenness to tell us that there was much excessive drinking. In the eighteenth century the Archbishop of York ruled that priests should not eat or drink in taverns.

The so-called Dark Ages and the reigns of Saxon kings saw the establishment of ale-houses and taverns that was to lead to today's public houses. The number grew rapidly, selling mostly home-brewed ale and mostly run by women, known as brewsters or ale-wives.

By the 1300s ale selling was still on a very small scale. We can safely conclude that the accommodation was only the ale-house kitchen and the only facility a warm fire. Because of the limitations, most sales must have been off the premises. Because there was so much poverty it was very likely that some ale-wives were driven to brewing and selling ale from necessity; they could possibly earn a little at harvest time, or when the price of barley made brewing worth while.

With an increase in the population and better wages, a rising demand gave ale-houses selling a good ale an opportunity to grow; food and social activities began to be offered, especially in towns. To mark these permanent ale-houses the use of ale-stakes – a pole with a bush at the end – became common and was soon made a requirement. In the 1400s the official licensing of ale-houses was introduced. By then the pattern of England's drinking houses was becoming clear:

Inns   These were the smallest in number, but largest in size, with the best standard of accommodation and widest range of food and drink. When coach travel brought passengers who needed overnight accommodation, it was the inns that provided it and offered stabling for horses. These coaching inns are easily recognised even today; an example is the Coach & Horses at Whitefield.

Inns became the focus for the social life of wealthy residents. They were the venues for balls and assemblies so beloved of Jane Austen's characters, and places where the local hunt would meet. Their size (often the largest building in the area after the church) made them suitable for business and council meetings; their locations encouraged their use by carriers for collections and deliveries. Their courtyards, stables and outbuildings made excellent commercial sense. Because of their quality, style and size, many of them were able to continue, successfully retaining their traditional role as inns. Others, aspiring to higher things, adopted the title 'hotel'. Either way, this was the quality end of the market.

Taverns   Lower down the social order and providing drinking facilities for upper-middle-class customers, taverns sold wine and basic food, but rarely offered accommodation. Once the railways had arrived the place of taverns in the scheme of things would be clearer with neighbouring establishments known respectively as the Station Hotel and the Station Tavern.

Taverns had a good deal of competition from higher-quality ale-houses and from coffee-houses in their age of popularity; eventually numbers began to fall and they began to lose a separate identity. By 1800 few taverns could be distinguished from ale-houses.

By the eighteenth century there was little difference between smaller inns, taverns and ale-houses. At the same time a new name began to cover most of this group: the 'public house', possibly through some sort of recognition of its place as a 'public ale-house'. This would have acknowledged its uniqueness as a private home, yet open to the public for the sale of ale. From the earlier, primitive one room and fire, many pubs, especially in towns, provided a parlour and a bar, vault or taproom. Social activities now increased, both in the pub and outside.

Ale-houses and early pubs had a very limited range of drinks, mainly ale, although cider and perry, for example, were available in districts in the west of England. The introduction of hopped beer from Flanders altered all that; the first recorded beer import was in 1400 in Sussex and its popularity quickly spread, particularly in the south. By 1600 beer had replaced ale in most pubs; the introduction of hops to the usual brewing ingredients of water, malt and yeast allowed a wide variety of flavours and strengths to be produced.

The brewing of beer was well suited to large-scale production, encouraging commercial brewing and giving a cheaper product. In the north, ale-house keepers continued to make their own drink for longer than in the south, but change was bound to come, not least because in its keeping properties beer had a longer product life than ale. In later years an unusually large quantity of hops was used for beer brewed for export: IPA (India Pale Ale) was a beer brewed in this way especially to take advantage of the preservative effect of the hops. Greene King Brewery had in mind the long sea voyage to India, where in the days of empire there was a big British expatriate market and a strong thirst! Eventually only the lightly hopped drink continued to be called ale, while the more heavily hopped version was called beer. There is no such distinction today.

Pub signs and their meaning

We have seen how a bunch of vine leaves or an ale-stake was once a sign denoting a drinking place. This was not only a convenience for travellers, but ensured that the premises were visited by the official ale-taster or ale-conner, whose duty was to test the quality and price of ale sold there. An ale-garland in the form of a wreath of flowers was added when a new brew needed the ale-conner's inspection.

Ale-house windows were often covered by lattice work or trellis, usually painted red: going back as far as the days of Elizabeth I these were a clear sign of an ale-house, but have long since ceased to be used for the purpose.

As the number of ale-houses increased, so the need to distinguish one from another for reasons of competition became stronger. From the simplest painted sign fixed to the front wall to elaborate hanging signs sometimes mounted in patterned wrought iron, the range is enormous. In medieval times and earlier few people were literate, so the name of the landlord or the ale-house on the sign would have been of little help; the reason for many of the ale-houses' chosen names is often obscure, but a fascinating study.

The most common names and signs today are thought to be: Red Lion, Rose and Crown (or Crown) and Royal Oak. At the White Bull at Ribchester there is a reproduction white bull prominently displayed high up in addition to a painted hanging sign, while a bunch of grapes on the front of the Swan and Royal at Clitheroe is a reminder of the vine leaves once used to mark drinking houses and the quality of the drink sold there.

Sad to say, very few examples remain of the spectacular 'gallows' signs that once stretched right across the road like football posts and crossbar. One by one they were demolished because of the expense of maintenance and the danger to passers-by. The most remarkable was that at the White Hart, Scole, now the Scole Inn, near Diss in Norfolk, erected in 1655 and held to be 'the noblest signe-post' in the country.

A fine survivor is at Barley on the Hertfordshire/Cambridgeshire border where at the Fox & Hounds a beam crossing the road carries on it the hunt in silhouette, showing the huntsmen closing in on the fox. Another once thought lost for ever has recently been replaced after a long fight. Brought down by a high-sided vehicle, the Magpie sign that crossed the A140 Norwich road at Stonham in Suffolk is back in all its glory; some of us may recall that the original carried the Brewery's name 'Tolly' below the bird. Such is everyone's satisfaction and pleasure in a battle won, the replacement Magpie alone on its new beam has been welcomed back unreservedly.

No mistaking the White Hart at Scole, near Diss in Norfolk, now the Scole Inn! The landlord must have been desperate to impress his guests to have been willing to pay £1,000 in 1655 for this elaborate sign. The whole structure is loaded with extravagant carving and has twenty-five life-size figures; in the centre of the arch is the white hart from which the inn originally took its name. The present sign is handsome and hangs over the road, but was far less costly.

The Magpie sign at Stonham in Suffolk is more basic than that at Scole, but is well loved locally. The pub and sign photograph well together, but patience is needed to capture a good moment and care as well, as the A140 traffic moves fast.

Ale-tasting: the tradition today

Everyday life in medieval England was originally administered through courts based on the historic manors around which settlements, including market towns, grew.

Henley-in-Arden in Warwickshire has one of the very few remaining manorial courts: its Court Leet. Today it represents little more than tradition and civic dignity, but its annual election of officers in November and its long record of their responsibilities and functions is a vital part of Henley's identity. Had it not been for Henley's ability to prove regular meetings of the Court Leet and Court Baron over many years, an Act of Parliament in 1976 would have abolished them, and the ale-tasting tradition as well.

The Henley Ale-taster is one of the Court's officers with robe and badge that have always marked the importance of his office. The first record of the Court in Henley was in 1333, but of special interest is a written statement of the Taster's duties dated 13 October 1593:

> We order that all the Ale Howse Kepers and Victelers within the liberties shall make good and holsome ale and beare for mans bodie and that they and every one of them sell the same for two pence half penny a gallon new and three pence stale and everyone denying to sell as aforesaide shall forfett for every offence XIId.

Henley's charter dates back to 1220, when Henry III granted Peter de Montfort, Lord of the Manor, the right to hold a weekly market and an annual fair at the feast of St Giles (1 September).

Giles was born at Athens; after the death of his parents he went to France, where he led the life of a hermit in a cave near the mouth of the river Rhone. After building a monastery there he became its first abbot. He was patron of cripples, lepers and nursing mothers; his churches (well over 100 were dedicated to him in England) are often at crossroads so that travellers halting for refreshment or for their horses to be shod could pray at church for a safe journey.

In the thirteenth century it was the custom on a market or fair day for the members of the Court Leet at Henley to parade around the town to warn all rogues, vagabonds and idle and disorderly persons to depart. They were to remain at their peril. Other courts existed at Alcester, Bromsgrove and Warwick so alternatives for the undesirables were limited. A very close relationship exists between these courts today, and invitations are exchanged welcoming representatives to their respective events.

Ale-tasting at Henley follows a ceremonial on a prearranged May evening; members of the Court Leet assemble and walk, robed, down the mile-long High Street, visiting in turn the eight pubs remaining there. There were double that number when the present Ale-taster was a schoolboy. At each pub the members of the Court are offered a half-pint of ale, which the Taster sips, pauses, considers

Rivington Hall.

carefully, then sips again, pronouncing meanwhile on the essentials such as flavour
and colour.

The Taster says that the ceremonial follows a well-established script. In
conclusion, the licensee is presented with a certificate of satisfaction and the Court
moves on to the next pub. It sounds like a pleasant social occasion, perhaps a
deserved compensation for the time devoted by the Court members to their various
duties. An additional Ale-taster has been appointed at Henley, allowing for an
increase in the membership of the Court Leet.

The description of ale tasting given on pp. 170–3 under the Plough at Eaves may
be closer to history as it really was than the highly coloured version of today at
Henley-in-Arden. But the contrast between the 'breeches test' as at the Plough and
the ceremonial at Henley is only to be expected; after all, much time has passed and
much else has changed, too.

AFFETSIDE NEAR BURY: *THE PACK HORSE*

Affetside: M60 to J15, Bolton A676 to Edgworth–Tottington crossroads. Turn sharp right for Affetside; or M60 to J18, M66 to J2, Bury A58 west along ring road. Turn right on to B6213 towards Tottington and fork left almost immediately for Affetside.

Little need for a postcode for this pub. What a historic address: 52 Watling Street! That was the name of the Roman road that ran all the way from the Romans' landing place at Richborough in Kent to Wroxeter near Shrewsbury and passed through Affetside on the stretch between Manchester and Ribchester, where there is a crossing of the Ribble.

This important road, built by the legions, was increasingly used as the centuries passed by merchants who needed to move goods such as cloth for sale at distant markets. Packhorse trains would have toiled up the hills here; Affetside stands on the highest local point, so the appropriately named Pack Horse was well located to provide shelter and refreshment for travellers. Today's visitors come by car and can linger to enjoy marvellous distant views such as Winter Hill.

Successive landlords of the Pack Horse have needed to increase their dining space. Apart from the main lounge bar at the front, there is a games room with dining tables near the entrance and a 'snug' by a side bar; access through the side bar

Standing on the Roman Watling Street, the Pack Horse has provided refreshment for travellers for hundreds of years.

allows diners to go through to two more dining rooms at the rear where the kitchen is located. At weekends every table is taken.

A feature at the Pack Horse which is remembered by everyone who visits it is the skull which is on a shelf at the back of the main bar. Bizarre and gruesome, it is that of George Whewell (variously spelt), a local man whose family was massacred by Royalist soldiers commanded by James, 7th Earl of Derby, at the time of the siege of Bolton during the Civil War.

An account in the form of a poem at the Pack Horse tells of the Royalists' defeat by Cromwell at Wigan, then again at Worcester, after which the King and Derby fled. The Earl was captured at Chester, tried and sentenced to death. He was sent back to Bolton where so many had died at the hands of the soldiers: Whewell volunteered as an executioner and gained his revenge.

One explanation of the display of Whewell's skull in the pub is that the Royalist soldiers came back to make him pay for executing their commander. His skull was said to have been displayed outside to warn everyone; eventually it was taken inside, where it remains. Needless to say there are numerous stories describing the horrific experiences of people who attempted to move the skull out of the Pack Horse. In publicity terms, the skull is better than the usual ghost only seen by a few select believers; the skull is there for all to see. It is also well positioned to see what is going on at the bar: just try to forget it is there!

Across the road and no more than 50 yards away there is evidence of the village's history. To celebrate the year 2000 a Millennium Green has been established, including a garden with pool and ducks: a so-called 'breathing space' with public footpaths giving people an opportunity to wander. The Rotary Clubs of Bolton have promoted a 50-mile circular walk, 'The Rotary Way'. A notice announces the start of Stage 1, from Affetside to Little Lever, 5¾ miles.

By the roadside nearby, facing a row of cottages, is the Affetside Cross. Heavily pitted, it stands on a plinth consisting of two circles of huge stones fastened together with metal straps. The shaft has a socket cut into the top which originally probably supported a cross, now lost; it would have served as

The Affetside Cross.

a market cross for Affetside and district, and was possibly a place for preaching and public proclamations. This form of standing cross would have been quite common in medieval villages, but most were destroyed during the sixteenth and seventeenth centuries, making the Affetside Cross a relatively rare survival. It is listed as an Ancient Monument, and tradition dates it as Roman, possibly because it marks the line of the Roman road. It may be Saxon or even medieval; both are more likely than Roman. A continuation of Watling Street can be seen north-west of Edgworth, but there is no cross on that length. The cross at Affetside is said to have a special significance as it is exactly half-way between London and Edinburgh.

One wonders how much that half-way position really matters – except perhaps to the people of Affetside. What does matter is transportation in such a scattered landscape, both public and private. There is a bus service to and from Bolton and there are parking bays on the narrow Watling Street close to the Millennium Green and the Affetside Cross. For patrons of the Pack Horse there is a good car park, excellent food and, of course, the famous skull of George Whewell.

ARKHOLME (KIRKBY LONSDALE ROAD)
THE REDWELL INN

A6 or M6 north to Carnforth. Turn east on B6254, Market Street, leading into Kellet Road and Kirkby Lonsdale road. The pub is beyond Over Kellet.

Why the official address of the Redwell Inn is given as Arkholme is one of life's mysteries. Perhaps it is something to do with the postcode. Don't look for it in the village, as it isn't there; watch for it on the Kirkby Lonsdale road well on the way

By early evening the pub car park was filling rapidly, a sure sign of the popularity of the Redwell Inn.

to Over Kellet. There will be plenty of cars at the front, such is the pub's popularity; fortunately there is plenty of space. Its sign is eye-catching, brilliantly glowing and illustrating the pub's red well from which it takes its name.

Like so many country pubs that have a long history, the Redwell was once a farm as well as an inn. The building goes back to the seventeenth century and later served travellers as a coaching inn: the archway on the front is evidence of that, as are the outbuildings at the rear, which would have been stables. A barn was often an extension to these farmhouse inns and was so here, but is now converted into a handsome, spacious dining and function room.

Food is the focus here. Choose your evening according to its speciality: Monday is steak night, Thursday is duck night, Friday is fresh fish night and so on. Food is on offer every day from 12 to 9 p.m.; one of the most popular dishes is Cumbrian roast lamb.

Well before eating out in the evenings became regular and car travel made it easy, the Redwell was an important place for people to meet socially and, of course, to drink together. It had an official function, too, as a courthouse, and served business as an auction room.

The present landlady at the Redwell, Julie, has recorded a number of stories or legends connected with the pub. Sadly this is all too rare, and when the story tellers are no longer around the stories may be lost for ever. She mentions the return visit of a former German prisoner of war who worked at the Redwell during the Second World War; he spoke highly of his treatment and how well he was fed.

Of past landlords, Matt Slaughter seems to have been ready to ignore food regulations in 1945. He became famous for his quick thinking when police came to inspect the premises in the belief that he was trading bacon when it was rationed. They didn't find the pig they thought was involved, as Matt had put it in bed with his wife!

A really poignant legend is that of Jack and Bess, the Redwell version of the willow-pattern plate story. It was 1685 when the Redwell stable boy Jack was found to be having a secret love affair with Bess, the daughter of the local master of the hunt. In spite of several warnings as to the serious consequences if Jack did not end the relationship, love seems to have been too strong and the affair continued.

The master of the hunt was known to be a heavy drinker and of a cruel disposition. One night when cock fighting was going on in the cellar at the Redwell and he was present, having had plenty to drink, news was brought to him that Jack and Bess had been seen. He ordered his men out, caught the lovers together and had Jack tied up. Despite Bess's distress and pleas to her father, a large fire was built and Jack was burned at the stake. The message to poor Bess was 'you are not to marry below your class and a gentleman of fine standing will be found for you'.

It is said that the experience of seeing Jack's death robbed Bess of the power of speech and she sobbed continually for twelve months before dying of a broken heart at the age of eighteen. On a clear night under a full moon Jack and Bess can be seen walking hand in hand down the lane by the Redwell Inn whispering their love for each other. The story ends by saying that they will not notice you: they have eyes only for each other.

The well giving the Redwell its name is still there under a modern cover close to the back of the pub. For some unknown reason way back in the past the well water is said to have suddenly turned red; the easiest explanation at the time was witchcraft. Today we would look for some change in the soil through which the water filtered.

Certainly, like the famous Chalice Well at Glastonbury, the water at the Redwell gained the reputation of having strange healing properties. A recent letter received at the pub from a lady in Canada aged ninety-one confirms this.

As a baby barely a year old she became seriously ill with what sounds like pneumonia. When the doctor came he

The well that gave the pub its name.

told the family that she was dying and would not see the night out. With nothing to lose, and led by her grandmother, the ladies of the house drew water from the well, warmed it on a stove and put it in a pan by the baby's bed. A towel was spread in the water, the baby was laid on the towel and she was bathed and soaked in the warm water. The ladies worked all night keeping the baby warm and clearing mucus from her nose and throat with a goose feather dipped in goose grease.

Next morning there was laughter and tears: the baby was well and is living ninety years on. She says now that her life was saved entirely because of the power of Redwell water and that it has always helped to build healthy teeth and bones for children there. One of these days perhaps the mystery of the red well will be solved, but if not, we have a ninety-year-old story with a happy ending.

Arkholme village is worth a visit – even Kirkby Lonsdale is only 4 miles further on. Turn at the Arkholme crossroads down to the river Lune and the church. There is no through traffic so the peace and quiet allows visitors to admire the stone cottages, Georgian houses and delightful gardens. The beautiful little church stands by an

The base of the ancient market cross close to the church at Arkholme.

The river Lune below Arkholme church. Along the riverside walks are willow trees that once provided material for the village's cottage industry, basket making.

ancient earthwork above the river and the remains of the old market cross are by the south side of the church.

Past the Ferryman's house a track leads quickly down to the riverside and its walks. This was the source of material, willow, for Arkholme's traditional cottage industry, now gone: basket making.

Stay on long enough for time to go to Kirkby Lonsdale, which affords wonderful views of the Lune valley.

John Ruskin, who knew a thing or two about the countryside, called it 'one of the loveliest scenes in England – therefore in the world'. The artist J.M.W. Turner painted the scene from a point close to the church there. They can't both be wrong!

BACUP AND THE COCONUTTERS: *THE CROWN INN*

M60 to J18, M66, A56, A681 via Rawtenstall; or M65 to J8, A56, A681 via Rawtenstall.

The father with a little boy asked 'Have the Nutters gone past yet?' There were people waiting about, some for buses, others looking anxiously at watches, so possibly something was expected. The father and son relaxed.

It was on St James Street near the library in the centre of Bacup on the Saturday of Easter weekend. Then the penny dropped. This is the one day in the year when the Britannia Coconut Dancers come to town to perform their ancient dances at every Bacup boundary – and at all the pubs on the way. If the number of pubs really matters, some say 'about twelve', others 'probably fifteen'. Since the Nutters get free beer at all of them, perhaps some uncertainty about the exact number is understandable. The Nutters say that they lose a lot of body fluid walking and dancing many miles and need to replace it!

As the crowds grew that day, including groups with walking boots and backpacks – certainly not locals – and many young people whose interest would usually be in something 'cool' rather than in tradition, the Britannia Coconut Dancers were a unique spectacle. But what makes these men of mature age black their faces so that the Devil cannot recognise them, don white hats decorated with red, white and blue rosettes, black jerseys, red-and-white kilts, white stockings and black Lancashire clogs?

They go on to perform dances accompanied by members of Sacksteads Silver Band and collect for charity. Ask one of the Nutters why they do it and keep to the same route every year. 'It has always been so; it is a way of life.' Their leader, Richard Shufflebottom, joined the Coconutters at age twenty-two; he retired in 2005 after fifty years. The Secretary, Joe Healey, has a tattoo on his arm that says 'Coconutter Born & Bred'.

More about the Coconutters later, but with their experience, surely a recommendation of a Bacup pub for inclusion in this book would be very simple. But nothing ever is. Remember the free beer for them at every pub along the way? This

The Coconutters in action.

The Crown Inn, Bacup. Don't look for an inn sign under the ivy – there isn't one.

poses a diplomatic problem, the only solution being careful detective work to find a way forward.

Every weekend from Easter to September the Coconutters are out and about dancing at carnivals, folk festivals and charity functions of all kinds. Where are they to be found when they are back home, have washed off their black and have taken off their 'gear'? Answer: at the Crown, which they seem to have made their own, bringing their wives and partners, also adding their own special brand of togetherness to the friendly informality of hosts Trevor and Kathy. A powerful combination!

Do not give up on your search for the Crown. There is no sign on the hill climbing out of Bacup along Yorkshire Street; look for Greave Road, fork right here and watch for a pub with no sign on the wall. A few parked cars give a clue, but the only other evidence is a tiny notice in a window partly hidden by ivy; all it says is Crown Inn, Greave Road, Bacup. Mon-Fri 5 p.m., Sat & Sun 12 noon. East Lancs Pub of the Year 2003 CAMRA.

Greave is a small community on the edge of Bacup, but the pub's regulars know it, love it and come from a wide area – and not just because of the quality of its beer. It is the quality of the company there that counts and reflects the personalities of Trevor and Kathy. Trevor has been landlord for more than eighteen years and his father before him for thirteen years.

They have kept a thick ring-file full of historical facts, illustrated with scores of photographs, all of which show how active and entertaining the pub has been during their years there. Records go back to 1866 when the Crown was owned by John Baxter Ltd of Glen Top Brewery at Bacup and James Lord was the licensee.

Changes have been many since then. James Lord would be astonished to know that on Thursday evenings the Bare Arts Class meets upstairs in the function room to paint and draw, but then Kathy is a professional artist. Trevor and Kathy also have a gallery with exhibits for sale at Todmorden called Bare Arts.Com. with its own website and Trevor plans to set up his own brewery nearby.

That is not all: every couple of weeks there is music – live music – in the Crown. It all started when a group of local musicians occasionally played in the pub and Trevor gave them free sandwiches. The group decided to go public and adopted as their entertainment name 'The Free Sandwiches'. Now fame is beckoning.

In the summer there is folk music at the Crown, a weekend festival, and the popular black pudding competition. Trevor feels that throwing black puddings is a waste of good food. If you are looking for a sandwich to beat all sandwiches, ask for one of Trevor's. They are on wholemeal bread with fillings to gladden the eye, such as roast beef with onion and horseradish or mustard. Mine had a printed label that said 'The Crown Inn, The Butty, Beef, £2.50' and satisfied my appetite until the following day. If your wish is a drink that is different you will find it at the Crown, because Trevor has two beers brewed specially for him at the Pictish Brewery at Rochdale.

The L-shaped bar has blazing fires at opposite ends, with two rooms opened out at the left-hand side of the bar, all facing the front. Country style-chairs, wooden topped

Interior of the Crown Inn, meeting place of the Coconutters and their many friends.

tables and a flagged floor set the tone. But if you make a first visit to the Crown, you will not be a stranger for long. Trevor, Kathy and their regulars will see to that and there will be a chair pulled out for you immediately.

To end with the Coconutters, their origin is believed to go back to the days when Moorish pirates settled in Cornwall and were employed in the mines there. Some came to Lancashire in the eighteenth and nineteenth centuries as mines were opened in the north, bringing the dances with them. Of those early groups, only the Britannia Coconutters are left. Their own evidence goes back to 1857.

The dancers blacken their faces to prevent their being recognised by evil spirits and one of the group, known as the 'Whiffler' or 'Whipper-in', walks in front of the dancers cracking his whip to drive evil spirits away.

The routine of the dancers begins with the garland dances, in which each member carries a garland decorated in red, white and blue to resemble flowers, part of the spring ritual. The Nut Dances follow and involve the use of wooden discs like coconut shells fixed to palms, knees and waists; dancers strike them together in time with the music, originally that of the English concertina. The so-called coconuts would, in the past, have served as a protection for the miners as they crawled down passages in the mines.

It seems so natural that the tradition and survival of the Britannia Coconut Dancers should have become linked with the custom of their pub visits on the Easter Sunday boundary-to-boundary trail at Bacup. Much of our past finds its expression in today's world through the English public house.

BELMONT: *THE BLACK DOG*

M60/M61 to Bolton, then A666 Blackburn road. Just after crossing Crompton Way fork left, A675.
From Blackburn A674, Preston Old Road, to M65, J3. Cross over motorway, then A675 Bolton road.

If wild open country and scenery are your pleasure, you will enjoy the West Pennine Moors. That is the setting for Belmont, often described as an industrial village, a label that is undeserved. One might expect to see chimneys in large numbers, mills (often derelict), run-down railways, neglected canals and poor, congested housing. Not at Belmont, although approaching from Bolton you will see the one large chimney, that of the dye and bleach works away to the right, nothing more industrial.

Opposite the Black Dog at the bottom of the steep High Street is Maria Square, with 1804 on its street sign and the most delightful stone cottages on its left side. Decorated with flowers, they lead down to the green, lined at the bottom with much more costly modern detached houses with colourful front gardens. Behind the trees is the dye and bleach works; many villagers must have come this way to work every day. Now it is the only active industrial unit in Belmont.

Look for the church and you will usually find the pub. This is so with the Black Dog at Belmont.

The Black Dog stands at the crossroads, an ideal position for business, a large car park opposite, just where it needs to be. Built in 1750, as a farm it remained so until 1825 when it was converted into a tavern brewing its own beer and has been an inn ever since. The Holt's Brewery of Manchester took over the pub in 1952.

With one exception, all the dining areas (three small rooms) face Church Street; at the far left is the kitchen and to the far right on the corner is the function room that will seat up to sixty diners. From across the road by the church wall the Black Dog looks very 'farmhousy', particularly at the kitchen end where a large arched gateway would have allowed farm carts into the courtyard. The pleasant flagged outdoor space has a magnificent yellow potentilla: a real prizewinner!

Someone in the past must have enjoyed collecting tankards and pint pots; every beam has them and all the walls have displays of countryside photographs and prints. Fishing is a favourite local pastime and a popular activity for visitors; the reservoirs round Belmont offer good fishing and permits are on sale at the pub, where professional fly-casting tuition can be arranged. The three bedrooms at the Black Dog are well booked by people working temporarily in the area and by tourists.

In spite of the climb, it is worth the walk to the top of the village for the view across Belmont Reservoir and the Sailing Club. Not only that, but nineteenth-century cottages along the High Street are a picturesque reminder of Belmont's prosperous days in the first half of the century. The depression in the second half of the nineteenth century, particularly in textiles, forced people in Belmont to look for work elsewhere and move away. In small building developments off the High Street are many modern houses; the lovely countryside has been a magnet for people preferring village life to that in town, and Belmont has continued to grow and prosper in recent years.

There is one other pub on the way up the hill, and the village post office. The range of merchandise on sale there is quite astonishing: if you need a bag of flour or a box of detergent, the post office will save you a long journey to a supermarket. Although the postmaster has no immediate competition, he provides an admirable service. On a tiring morning with no teashop or coffee bar for miles he said, 'I can make you a takeaway coffee!' He did and it was a lifesaver. Without him I would not have found Potato Pie Walk at the top of Ryecroft Lane. Its name recalls the potato pie supper that marked the success of the village campaign to preserve a right of way down to the recreation ground. Exercise that right: at the bottom cross Rivington Road (leading into Church Street and back to the Black Dog) and walk over the playing field. Then do what the villagers do. Sit on one of the seats on the bank of Ward's Reservoir, or locally Ward's Lodge, and enjoy a fabulous view over the water and up to the summit of Winter Hill, 1,500 feet high, with its TV mast.

St Peter's Church, opposite the Black Dog, dates from 1850 and is in fine condition. Close to the porch and below the clock is a recent addition, a bust of Gerald Ashmore wearing his trilby. Where it is usual to find a saint or bishop, or a gargoyle, Belmont has Gerald. He served St Peter's in so many ways and for so long that people wanted to thank him. Get into conversation at the Black Dog and someone is sure to ask 'Have you seen Gerald yet?' People are valued here: in the pub is an extract from an 1872 issue of the *Bolton Chronicle* giving an appreciation of the life of Benjamin Helme of Belmont who took over the Black Dog after working on the Belmont estate. He also served as Overseer and Surveyor of Highways.

The bar at the Black Dog, just beginning to swing into action.

Gerald Ashmore wearing his trilby.

Potato Pie Walk at Belmont, the right of way preserved following a local campaign.

When Belmont fell on hard times in 1860 he tried in many ways to bring life back to the village and pressed for the construction of a railway to Belmont. He built sixteen homes for working people, but the village became almost deserted and with one exception his houses stood empty for over ten years.

At the bottom of the village is Hordern Brook; the village shared this name, but 'Hordern' is unattractive, particularly when spoken by the locals, sounding like 'Hard Earn'. So, led by employers, the name was changed in 1804 to Belmont. One wonders if the name change influenced people: it certainly impressed me!

Just opposite the Black Dog is a signpost at the crossroads: Belmont is about half-way between Bolton and Blackburn, but of immediate and very local interest is the 3¼ miles to Rivington past the front of the pub. Lancastrians travel many times that distance to visit Rivington and the gardens of Lever Park, named from William Hesketh Lever, later Lord Leverhulme, who bought the estate in 1900. Rivington Hall itself was included, also ancient barns which he restored and are used now for the convenience of visitors. His terraced gardens above the park comprise about 45 acres of waterfalls, ornamental pools and a new woodland with many varieties of trees and thousands of shrubs.

Above it all is Rivington Pike, 1,192 feet high, once a beacon site; the beacon is said to have been lit in 1588 as a warning that the Spanish Armada had been sighted. When visiting the Black Dog do not miss Lever Park at Rivington: Lord Leverhulme intended it to be for the benefit of the general public.

BISPHAM GREEN: *THE EAGLE AND CHILD*

M6 to J27, then A5209 west. From Parbold Hill turn on to B5246, Lancaster Lane. Continue via Crimshaw Green; turn left for Bispham Green

The address of the Eagle and Child is frequently given as Parbold; it may be to avoid confusion with Bispham in the Fylde, but if it reminds people that going to Bispham Green would give them a chance of visiting the viewpoint at the top of Parbold Hill on the way to the Eagle and Child, they have a real bonus. The view is tremendous: down below is the river Douglas, while the countryside stretches out to Ashurst's Beacon and the country park surrounding it to the distant horizon and Skelmersdale.

The Eagle and Child stands exactly where it should be: at the village crossroads, and looks as if it has been there a very long time. Built in the 1750s, every piece of visible evidence shows it to have been a farmhouse originally. As soon as you park your car in the rear parking area, the outbuildings and the working yard tell immediately of farm activity. The building added to the house itself with outside steps leading to an upper floor, suggests stables and possibly a hayloft above.

Entering by the back door from the courtyard at the end of the bar, the original family living room is opposite, on the left-hand side of the front entrance and looking out on to the road. The open-plan bar area would have been the workplace – possibly a dairy? Up several steps is the expected extension, called the Stables, set with tables for evening meals. The floor is of huge flags, carpeted beyond the bar, furnished in a country style including antique oak settles, and decorated with hops.

The farmhouse that became a pub. Its uncommon name comes from a legend that tells of a baby found in an eagle's nest.

The rear of the Eagle and Child. Perhaps the barn to the left was a hayloft and stables.

The popularity of the Eagle and Child can be judged by the listings it has been given and awards it has achieved. In the *Good Pub Guide 2005* it was listed as Lancashire Dining Pub of the Year; in *Period Living* and *Traditional Homes* it was a finalist in Best Country Pub 2004–2005 and Steve Prescott was nominated Pub Chef of the Year, 2004.

Apart from the obvious high quality of food on offer, the pub has an annual beer festival in May that includes live music. The rear wild garden is a permanent attraction, also the bowling green, which no doubt baffles many visitors unfamiliar with crown green bowling.

The Eagle and Child pub sign is not a common one, the great majority being in Lancashire, and is sometimes known as 'Bird and Bantling'. It refers to the Stanley family, earls of Derby, and derives from the legend of Sir Thomas Lathom, a fourteenth-century ancestor of the Stanleys, whose marriage was childless. He had an illegitimate son by a village girl and a plan was concocted to adopt the child as his heir. It is said that Sir Thomas and Lady Lathom regularly walked through the forest on his estate and, having placed the baby in an eagle's nest, Sir Thomas persuaded his wife that it had been left by the eagle so that she would regard the infant as a gift from God. Brought up by the Lathoms, the boy inherited the estate; his daughter married into the Stanleys, whose arms show the eagle above an infant in cloth wrappings. The pub sign at Bispham Green also carries the words '*Sans changer*' (without change).

One of the great treasures of the National Trust in Lancashire is within easy reach of the Eagle and Child: Rufford Old Hall. Built by Sir Thomas Hesketh in the sixteenth century, its timbered Great Hall is unaltered; its roof is divided into five

A view towards the stables at the Eagle and Child. Evening meals are served there up the steps. Someone loves King Charles spaniels.

Rufford Old Hall (National Trust). Spectacular inside and out, the lantern on the ridge of the roof of the Great Hall replaced the original louvre that allowed smoke from the central fireplace to escape.

bays of carved hammer beams and there is a massive bay window at the high-table end of the hall. At the lower, or service, end is a rare, richly carved portable screen 7 feet wide. There would have been a fireplace in the middle of the floor with a louvre to allow the smoke to escape; after a wall fireplace had been put in, the louvre was replaced by a 'lantern' on the ridge of the roof.

It would be worth a visit for the Great Hall alone, but there is much, much more, including a fine collection of furniture, arms and armour. Hesketh's players, his own group of actors, played in the hall and there is strong evidence that William Shakespeare was a member for some time having joined them from Hoghton Tower (see Hoghton Royal Oak, pp. 86–9).

From the Eagle and Child take Green Lane opposite, turn right into Rufford Road, cross the railway at Rufford station and turn right on A59T. Rufford Hall is a short distance on the right.

BLACKSTONE EDGE, LITTLEBOROUGH
THE WHITE HOUSE

A58, between Ripponden and Littleborough/Rochdale.

It was miserably cold and windy as only Pennine winters can be; the bar staff took pity on this photographer whose fingers could no longer handle the camera and opened the door early for him. The roaring log fire in the bar explained the huge stock of fuel piled up along the side of the 'wrap-around' car park of the White House. Standing 1,300 feet above sea level, with Yorkshire below to the east and

A welcome sight for travellers from east or west; today's White House on Blackstone Edge, close to the border of Yorkshire and Lancashire.

The White House in its days as the Coach and Horses. It must have been a welcome sight to eighteenth-century travellers.

Littleborough town in Lancashire to the west, the pub is a landmark for miles. The two counties' border is only a stones' throw away.

The building, white as its name suggests, dates from 1671 and was once a coaching house. An eighteenth-century journey across the Pennines would have been dangerous and very uncomfortable, so the Coach and Horses, as it was originally known, has been a welcome shelter for many years. Today walkers on the Pennine Way, which passes the pub, are grateful to see it, especially on a cold day. The White Horse publicity says the Coach and Horses is where in the past 'the young bloods of Littleborough having guarded the mail coach from highwaymen would seek recompense for their labours with the vigorous application to strong liquors'.

There was once a Baitings Inn near here, possibly somewhere on the old road, now straightened and properly paved. (Baitings were mealtimes, according to tradition, and the term is sometimes used even today.) It was not until a Turnpike Act was passed in 1735 that authority was given to repair and widen the road from Rochdale to Yorkshire. Celia Fiennes took the Blackstone Edge route in 1695 and Daniel Defoe did so in 1720; both did it the hard way, as their accounts make clear, and neither paid it any compliments.

Facing the A58 is the pub's main restaurant, surprisingly large for a location like this, but all is explained by 12.30 p.m., when the bar lounge called the Moorland Room is already full and overflowing into two other smaller dining rooms. The view from the Moorland Room is spectacular, with the central window table regularly reserved. The extensive 'specials' board has on its top line 'Bury Black Pudding and Mash'. What else? This is Lancashire.

The landlord admits to having a ghost, but only as an explanation for broken glasses. Legend goes further, telling of Frank Cropper, an early landlord, who must have wanted revenge on his customers after he died, having threatened to come back to haunt the place. He is blamed for switching off the cooker (did someone forget to switch it on?), for tables that move by themselves and boxes which fly across the kitchen. But Frank may not after all be the culprit: another explanation is that it is the ghost of a highwayman who attacked travellers on Blackstone Edge and kept his horse in the cellar. One wonders how much the landlord of that time knew of this.

All this is fairly trivial compared with the events of 6 December 1894, when a man called Robert Ackrigg arrived at the pub and ordered whisky which one of the girls served to him. Some time later he began shouting for the landlord; on his arrival Ackrigg demanded information about a lost dog. When the landlord insisted that he knew nothing of the dog, Ackrigg produced a gun and shot at him, wounding him in the arm. Fearing the worst, the landlady called for help, only to be shot too; fortunately the bullet was said to have been deflected by the steel of her corset (clearly a successful dual-purpose garment!). Ackrigg escaped but was soon caught; at his trial he was imprisoned for twelve years.

Littleborough, below the White House, had a Roman camp nearby, the Roman road from Manchester to York passing close to the town. It climbed up to Blackstone Edge near the line of a packhorse road; although it is not certain to have been made by a Roman legion, its skilled construction using local stone and its 16-foot width from kerb to kerb make it very likely.

The White House is close to the main access footpath to the Roman road and is worth a visit. Its condition is good, although stone robbing in the past has reduced its length. Of special interest and much controversy is the central trough. Several theories have been advanced to explain its use: a braking channel to stop runaways seems the most plausible.

It is lonely, wild country here, with ever-changing contours and virtually bare of trees. It is valuable countryside, though, for water catchment, and the reservoirs are vast. For the passionate walker it is a challenge and the White House is a haven, especially if the weather is unkind. The scenery is incomparable and there is a great sense of freedom. For the motorist it is a wonderful drive; for both, fine food awaits.

A warm corner at the White House to gladden the hearts of walkers on the Pennine Way.

BOLTON: *THE OLD MAN & SCYTHE*

Good trains from all parts, particularly Manchester Victoria and Piccadilly.
By road, M61 to J3, A666 St Peter's Way. At A579 turn left to town centre,
then right on Bradshawgate. Continue to Bank Street/Manor Street. Parking
below St Peter's Way; or M61, to J5; A58 Wigan Road into Deane Road, right
into Moor Lane, Trinity Street, pass Bolton Rail Station then Bradshawgate as
above. Pub near corner of Bradshawgate, Churchgate and Deansgate.

Some pubs create excitement and interest while they are still out of sight. It is the anticipation of discovery, looking forward to the unexpected; as the saying goes 'You learn something new every day'.

After a thirty-year absence I stood again on Churchgate. It was still there all right, the parish church just where I remembered it at the far end and the market obelisk at the corner, but almost all had changed in between. Gone was the Grand Theatre which opened in 1894 as a music hall; gone too, the Theatre Royal, demolished in 1963. Remember *The Maid of the Mountains?* What a show that was! Like both of them, many other properties have been demolished or converted, giving Churchgate a different look. It was once the marketplace, where everything happened, even a civil war action; John Wesley spoke here several times. People came here for food, drink and entertainment until the centre of business moved away beyond Deansgate; the Market Hall was built in 1855 and although it remained a busy thoroughfare, Churchgate's role was diminished.

The Old Man & Scythe: they don't come much older than this! It has to be Lancashire with a notice saying 'to t'yard'.

While we know the Old Man & Scythe was rebuilt in 1636, there is likely to have been an inn on the site as far back as 1251, when Bolton received its market charter; it certainly qualifies as the oldest pub in Bolton. Not only that, history was made here and has been recorded in some detail: the pub's black-and-white style, gables, windows and signs on the front walls promise a voyage of discovery.

The best starting point must be the pub sign; its derivation and the changing ownership of the land here is worthy of a special study. In early times the De Ferrers family were the landowners with the title Earls of Derby; through marriage the land passed to the Pilkingtons. In his book *Death: the Grim Reaper – the Pilkington Crest*, Malcolm Howe describes its derivation. The family's belief is that an ancestor who was fighting on the side of Richard III at the Battle of Bosworth Field in 1485 tried to avoid capture by taking up a scythe in a nearby field and pretending to be a labourer at work, saying to himself, 'Now thus, now thus.'

The pub's sign above the door shows the mower in a costume and hat of alternating colours: these would originally have been black and white. The owner's curious and unlikely grasp of the scythe is believed to explain why the so-called mower's disguise failed and he was taken prisoner. After Bosworth and Henry Tudor's victory, the Pilkingtons lost their lands at Bolton; the new king, Henry VII, rewarded the Stanley family, creating Thomas Lord Stanley, who had supported him, Earl of Derby. From then on the pub was in the ownership of the Earls of Derby.

Much at the Old Man & Scythe has changed since then, especially in 1636, when brick walls were introduced to replace those of medieval wattle-and-daub construction and the ancient cellar was altered. There were further alterations in the nineteenth century which included flagstones in the bar area to cover the early floor of ashes and cobblestones; an extension to the rear was made and now houses tables and chairs.

The bar stretches along the flagged corridor towards the rear with end bar counters to left at front and back. On the right of the corridor are two important rooms: that on the front looks out on what was once a busy market, while next along the corridor, facing rearwards, a room has a large plaque stating 'AW 1636'. There is a good decorated ceiling here and a glass cabinet which contains items of historical interest connected with the Civil War in the marketplace. It has naturally come to be known as the Museum Room.

Manchester and Bolton supported Parliament in the Civil War, together with Bury and Blackburn; the more rural areas were strongly Royalist. Two unsuccessful attacks were made on Bolton by Royalist troops in 1643 and March 1644, but on 28 May that year the defences were breached. In taking the town, the Royalist forces killed defenders and civilians without mercy in what became known as the Massacre of Bolton, mainly outside the Old Man & Scythe. The exact number of dead will never be known: we can be sure that at least 100 were killed, a huge number for a small town as it then was. The Earl of Derby was one of the Royalist leaders and was said to have killed a prisoner, for which, later, he was to pay with his own life.

In 1651 he was one of the Royalist commanders at the battle of Worcester, where a new king, Charles II, crowned in Scotland, hoped to restore the English monarchy. The battle was lost. Charles II became a fugitive, hunted by Cromwell's soldiers before escaping to France; the Earl of Derby was captured and taken to Chester to be tried. Found guilty, he was sentenced to be executed at Bolton: a sign on the wall of the Old Man & Scythe tells the story: 'In this ancient hostelry James Stanley Earl of Derby passed his last few hours of his life previous to his execution Wed. 15th Oct. 1651'. The chair on which the Earl sat waiting for his summons to the scaffold has been damaged, but can be seen in the glass-fronted cabinet in the Museum Room at the Old Man & Scythe.

The scaffold was on the site of the old market cross (where the nineteenth-century obelisk now stands) almost opposite the Old Man & Scythe. The executioner was James Whowell (or Whewell) from Edgworth, who was said to have lost his wife and

The Museum Room.

daughter after they were attacked by Royalist soldiers roaming in the country-side. His skull is lodged behind the bar at the Pack Horse, Affetside (see pp. 11–13). Each year there is an enactment outside the Old Man & Scythe at 3.00 p.m. on 15 October. In July there is an annual medieval fair.

People come from far and near to these events – even from overseas; these long-distance visitors would, surely, be puzzled by the Lancashire dialect and by some of the stories told using it. The Old Man & Scythe's shortened local name is 'T'Cider 'Ouse'. Cider is one of the specialities of the house; it's lightly coloured, semi-sweet and with a delicate aroma. Ask for Thatchers; minimum strength 6, so take care. It is very popular with the regulars, who drink it by the pint!

The obelisk at the corner of Churchgate.

If you think that a good 'trotter' is something to do with a pork meat dish, or is a nickname for a football team, read 'John o' God's Sending' (*Lass at the Man & Scythe*), a story of events at the pub by Allen Clarke, and on sale there. During an argument at the pub the landlord says 'Hoo had thee theer. Hoo would make a good trotter. Hoo would beat oaur Bowton trotters at their own sport.' Trotting was the pleasure of making a fool out of someone, particularly a stranger, by issuing a challenge that the trotter cannot lose.

A good trotting story tells of the pub regular who challenged a visitor saying that he would keep his foot in boiling water and would place a bet on it. What he did not say was that he had an artificial leg; of course, he won the bet, having tricked the visitor and qualified as a good 'trotter'.

If you are looking for a pub with a history and a reputation, look no further than the Old Man & Scythe.

BURNLEY: *THE OLD RED LION and THE SWAN INN*

From the north, M6, M61 to M65, J2.
From the south, M6 to J29, then M65; or M60 to M61, J9, then M65.

Seeking out a historic pub in the countryside is usually fairly simple: after all, pubs are likely to be at or near the centre of villages and are easily noticed. Not so in town centres, with congestion, one-way streets and parking problems.

Imagine, then, an alternative to the car. A fast, hourly rail service runs from Blackpool North, Preston, Blackburn and Accrington to York, calling at Burnley Manchester Road Station. Downhill, passing the fascinating Weavers' Triangle, the Inn on the Wharf, then the Town Hall, just follow Manchester Road to its junction with St James Street and there you are. On and around the corner are the Old Red Lion and its neighbour, the Swan. They could not be more different, so both are included here.

It seemed too good to be true to find that Leslie Chapples had already researched Burnley's pubs; his detailed work *The Taverns in the Town* was published by the Burnley & District Historical Society in 1986 and it is with the Society's permission that I quote from him where needful.

The Old Red Lion

This is one of the most popular pub names in the country, and hundreds remain today: John of Gaunt's badge was a red lion. He became Duke of Lancaster in the fourteenth century and although there is no historic connection between him and the establishment of the Burnley pub, the name is most appropriate here in Lancashire.

The Old Red Lion has a prominent position, seen from both Manchester Road and St James Street, and is well built and carefully preserved.

As a possible site for a new town hall in Burnley in 1865 it was unsuitable then and even more so today.

The spacious
bar area of the
Old Red Lion.

Chapples says, 'In 1865 the newly formed Burnley council bought the inn and actually had it demolished. At the time it was a suggested site for the new town hall, but the proposal was vetoed, with the result that in 1868 the hotel was rebuilt on its present site.'

Today the pub is immaculate; occupying, as it does, a large corner site, it commands attention. A modern refurbishment has created a single large open space with a central bar; round it is a wide band of tables and chairs in a horseshoe-shaped plan. Chapples tells us:

> The landlord most closely associated with the Old Red Lion was probably James Pate, a stage coach driver, who used the house as a centre for his coaching activities, driving his six horse stage to Manchester on Mondays and Thursdays and returning the following days. It seems that he had an understanding, responsible and energetic wife for on Mondays while he was away with his coach the inn yard became a pig market where farmers and tradesmen conducted their business. In addition to the landlord's coaching activities, other carriers used the inn's stabling facilities, with a regular service to Colne, departing at 9.00 a.m. during the week and a 10.00 a.m. departure on Sundays.

The Swan Inn

The Swan is very small compared with the Old Red Lion and has a number of small rooms off the modest bar. Its great age is clear from its external stonework, which probably dates to the sixteenth or seventeenth centuries. Internally a huge gash of plaster wall in the games room has been left bare to the stone because of restrictions on interior work in this listed building. Chapples again: 'It was a famous posting

A modest frontage, but two of the best inn signs in Lancashire.

house for coaches between Manchester and Skipton and had the honour of entertaining nightly the worthy trades-people of Burnley who would drop in for a market glass on Mondays and a nightcap on other evenings and discuss the latest news and prices.'

It was the custom for landlords of pubs to have other business interests. In the nineteenth century the then landlord, Kit Edmondson, farmed land close by and kept a butcher's shop near to the Swan. At one time a narrow room behind the bar was used to take coach bookings.

Don't miss the jail down the entry at the corner of the pub, they said. Sure enough, there it was, stone-walled with two barred windows built on to the back of the Swan. Lights on in the windows! It can't still be in use, can it? Read on.

Leslie Chapples wrote in picturesque language: 'In 1819 it was decided to

The old prison cells built on to the rear of the Swan Inn with entry from inside the pub – to the gents'.

utilise land in Red Lion Street to build a new jail, which was erected at the rear of the Old Red Lion and the Swan Inn and soon became known as "t' black 'oyle'". The prison was later transferred to Keighley Green police headquarters, but some of the cells remained and one of them is actually still in use – as the gents' toilet in the Swan! Be reassured, wall tiles and all mod cons are there, with a discreet entrance at the back of the bar area. Quite bizarre!

Small as it may be, the Swan is nevertheless an excellent candidate for inclusion in this book, not merely for the features already described: it has two external Swan signs that deserve a special mention. These and the blue plaque on the front wall should be enough to tempt any photographer to make extravagant use of his film.

CARNFORTH STATION and REFRESHMENT ROOM

M6 to J35, then A601M. For station take Market Street, cross at lights. From Lancaster A6, fork left Haws Hill (station sign). One-way traffic. Station on left at bridge. Good car parking at station.

There can be few who were born in the post-war years who do not remember *Brief Encounter*, a film whose story was of hopeless love and its consequences, starring Celia Johnson and Trevor Howard. Adapted from Noel Coward's *Still Life*, most of the action was based on a railway station, a chance encounter and the love that grew as the couple's meetings brought them ever closer together.

In 1945 a fictional station, Milford Junction, needed to be located well away from London, air raids and blackout problems; David Lean, the director, chose Carnforth. In the film, the trains used regularly by the lovers were on different lines and left within a short time of each other, but allowed them long enough to meet in the Refreshment Room and for their relationship to deepen. That Refreshment Room has been restored exactly to its appearance in wartime and its setting in the film.

The sad sight of the decaying premises of Carnforth station in the years that followed the railway closures of the 1960s caused many heartaches. It needed the vision of one man to believe in the possibility of a restoration and to put a plan for it into action. Like the creation of the Eden Project and the rebirth of the Lost Gardens of Heligan in Cornwall, Carnforth's future lay in the hands of one man: at Carnforth, Peter Yates, now honoured with an MBE.

He was able to see two powerful strands of feeling that could renew what was being lost through neglect. Carnforth was a railway town: over 800 men and women had been employed in the engine sheds, offices, and on the marshalling yards. There were also, of course, the footplatemen, who numbered 230. There was a strong sense of community and fellowship, particularly among those working on steam engines, the last of which were being decommissioned; a way of life was disappearing. A second strand, equally powerful, was represented by the thousands of men and women who had warm memories of Carnforth and still had gratitude for the kindness shown to them en route to embarkation for overseas service in wartime. Whatever the hour of day or night there were always volunteers at Carnforth with tea and sandwiches. For many this was the last stop and the last act of kindness before setting out to meet great danger.

If the two strands could be brought to a focus on what was being lost, Carnforth might yet be saved – and it was. The power of nostalgia itself was remarkable: the loyalty of volunteers in maintaining today's visitor centre is equally so. One unforeseen event was to play a big part in influencing the future: the film *Brief Encounter*.

Today's visitors will see the Refreshment Room just as Laura and Alec saw it; the clock which they dreaded to watch is there. There is no conventional pub sign, of course, just a notice saying Refreshment Room and Platform 1. The sight and sound of steam are missing, but the feeling of having been there before is uncanny. There is a wide-ranging menu, superb coffee and a good choice of alcoholic drinks.

This may not be a traditional pub in a marketplace, or on a village green, but the Refreshment Room stands on an island platform with rail tracks on each side – a unique

The restored bar at Carnforth just as it looked in the film *Brief Encounter*.

location with a unique atmosphere. It lacks the regulars of the 'local', but has an enormous pulling power for those who came this way in wartime and for families of that generation who have somebody to remember.

Sixty years or more is not a long time in pub history, but it is a long time for memories to bring people from all over the world to the visitor centre. The £1.8 million raised by the Carnforth Station and Railway Trust Co. Ltd, supplemented by lottery awards, was enough to refurbish the old Station Offices. They were converted to a visitors' centre with galleries that exhibit artefacts representing steam railways and the days of *Brief Encounter*.

Carnforth's platform clock: a reminder of Laura and Alec's brief meetings here.

A pride-of-place exhibit is George Nightingale's bowler hat. George was Shed Master and Area Transport Manager at Carnforth station from 1960 to 1983. Remember the days when bowlers were a mark of seniority?

The Visitor Centre was opened officially in October 2003 by Margaret Barton, who played Beryl in the film. If you wish to see *Brief Encounter* when you visit Carnforth, you can do that too. They made the film in the bitter early months of 1945 and Celia Johnson is quoted as saying that she grew fond of Carnforth station and its staff, though the arrival of the fish train from Aberdeen at 7.30 a.m. was not hugely popular.

It is worth adding that the guides will give you just as warm a welcome as any pub landlord – and there is no admission charge!

CATON: *THE SHIP INN*

M6 to J34, then A683 towards Kirkby Lonsdale.

Hot buttered toast recalls dark winter days and tea in front of the fire – at least it does to many of us. It has a resonance, a distant memory, just nostalgia perhaps. The landlord at the Ship knows exactly how important traditional menus and dishes like Lancashire hotpot and red cabbage are to people, and says that we forget that at our peril.

Hanging outside the pub is a painted sign of a great ship in full sail. Again, traditional, and a rather too obvious explanation for the pub's name. In fact, it took its present name from a local mill which produced sailcloth in the nineteenth century. In those days the area where the Ship and industry were located was

The Ship Inn at Caton: a traditional view of an unusual pub.

known as Townend; its mills took their power from the Artle Beck which fed into a mill race. Whether the Romans used the water for power or for supplies we do not know, but a massive Roman milestone was found there.

The history of the Ship is recorded as far back as 1680 and the pub recalls with pride the refreshment offered to travellers on this northern route. With the development of motorways and other trunk roads it is surprising how heavy the traffic flow is between Lancaster and Kirkby Lonsdale, thence, of course, to Kendal and the Lakes. There was a railway once; you will see an old-fashioned signal set at 'go' alongside the road to Claughton (just for fun, as the track was removed in 1968).

Caton's population dwindled after the mills at Townend closed: five in all, producing silk, cotton and flax at various times. Now the buildings have been converted for housing. In those busy days stage-coaches called at Caton; photographs at the Ship recall the history of the village and the part played by the pub. Where the beer garden now is, a grocer's shop stood, linked to the Ship. It was demolished in 1904, but the malthouse for the pub's own brew still stands at the opposite end, now a dwelling. There was a clog maker's too, but with the closure of the mills there was little business to be had.

Thirlmere Bridge is also a landmark in the village, as it carried water pipelines from Thirlmere to meet the needs of the growing city of Manchester. Caton's church is at Brookhouse – the other end of the village from the Ship; it was a quite separate village from Townend at one time, but the two settlements became joined 'between the wars'. The church tower is ancient, but the rest dates from the late nineteenth century.

The Ship does a magnificent job with its many historic photographs showing the pub, the grocer's shop and village life generally. Much has changed inside the pub to accommodate diners; there is a handsome overmantel with wonderful carving. 'Yes,' said the landlord, 'That is a Gillow piece.' Look carefully and you will see the keyholes of three cupboard doors, one in each panel; it was very nearly scrap as the backs of the cupboards were infested with woodworm. Only the doors from this unknown source could be saved – and what a mercy!

The food at the Ship is as traditional as Gillow furniture, and matches it in quality too. Thwaites Brewery gave the Ship their 'Supreme Kitchen' Award in 2004 and 2005; it was also a 'Best Kept Pub' Award winner and was included in the *Good Pub Guide* in 2004.

The Ship has been on the scene for many years, but facing the beer garden is something much, much older: the Old Oak Tree and the Fish Stones. The tree is twisted into a grotesque shape; it can hardly still be alive, but has a preservation order on it. Below are the famous Fish Stones, used by the monks from Cockersand Abbey near Lancaster who had the rights of salmon fishing on the river Lune. When they had a surplus they would bring fish to the stones and sell them to local people.

Caton's countryside attractions offer visitors a wide choice: the Trough of Bowland is not far away and Hornby is only a few miles in the Kirkby Lonsdale direction. There, the river Wenning joins the Lune; from the river bridge there is a spectacular view of Hornby Castle, once the home of John Foster, the Bradford textile manufacturer (remember Black Dyke Mills Band?).

Foster bought the Honour and Manor of Hornby in the nineteenth century; it is currently up for sale, but don't ask the price – you can't afford it!

Perhaps of all the choices for a visit my best recommendation would be the 'Crook o' Lune', very close to Caton. The river views there are quite stunning and the

Three beautifully carved cupboard doors fashioned into an overmantel in the Ship are believed to have originated at the Gillow workshop.

An unusual and very ancient market stall used by monks from Cockersand Abbey: the Fish Stones. Above and behind is the Old Oak Tree, hollow, but in spite of its twisted shape it seems to live on.

County Council makes visitors welcome by providing a car park and picnic site, refreshments in the summer and paved paths that lead to the beauty spots, to the river bank and places where you will use all your film. Special access is available for the disabled, even to reach the place where Turner did his famous painting. If you admire the view, you will be in good company – so did William Wordsworth.

CHURCHTOWN, SOUTHPORT: *THE BOLD ARMS*

From Preston A59/A565. At Churchtown/Marshside junction on A565, turn left, landmark Churchtown Medical Centre. Follow Cambridge road, keep left, pub on right opposite church.
From Liverpool A59, then A570T from Ormskirk.
From M6, J26, M58, J3, then A570T from Ormskirk.

Liverpool and M6 drivers: at Meols Cop Retail Park roundabout fork right, B5276. This is Meols Cop Road into Norwood Road/Avenue. At T junction turn right, B5269 Roe Lane. At next roundabout keep left, Mill Lane/Manor Road. Turn right into Cambridge Road at next roundabout. Pub on right opposite the church. It's easier than it sounds, and Churchtown is signposted at junctions.

'If only' is a phrase regularly used to explain how the course of events in our history has been transformed by some decision, apparently unimportant at the time. The Bold Arms at Churchtown and its celebrated landlord in 1776, William (Duke) Sutton, fit

A rural gem in tourist country. The Bold Arms at Churchtown and the neighbouring cottages go back to the seventeenth century.

The stocks at Churchtown.

nicely into this category, because if Sutton had not noticed the business potential of the growing popularity of sea bathing, Southport might never have happened.

Many of the regulars in the past at the Bold Arms were shrimpers; they lived close to the seashore, or on the margin of the salt marsh, which according to the present landlord meant the rim of the land. He says it explains why there are so many people in the village with the family name of 'Rimmer'.

The Bold Arms became a meeting place for fishermen at the crossroads by St Cuthbert's Church; the narrow one-way street of small shops in the centre there, the timbered and thatched cottages and the two remaining pubs go back to the seventeenth century. The site of the Bold Arms was probably that of an ale-house or tavern much earlier, as the title deeds of Robert de Meols in the reign of King John (1199–1216) has a mention of a 'place of entertainment' there.

Today, however, Churchtown is more like a suburb of sophisticated Southport but, mercifully, it has preserved its identity and links with its fishing-village past. Even the stocks remain, enclosed in the church-yard wall opposite the pub. The placard beside the stocks states that they were built by Robert Linaker in 1741 and that the last wrongdoer to be placed there was Thomas Rimmer on 3 June 1861; his sentence was six hours for drunkenness. For such a small village three pubs at that time seems excessive, perhaps even explaining Rimmer's condition. The Bold Arms was known in its early days as the Griffin or the Middle House, with the Farmer's Arms (now closed) on one side and the Black Bull on the other.

The two great landowners in the district were the Bolds and the Heskeths. The Bolds built a manor house on Manor Road (formerly Marshside Lane) in 1554; rebuilt in 1802, it was called Bold House. The Heskeths owned Rufford Hall; they also owned land at Churchtown, living at

One of the griffin panels at the back of the pub.

The former stables in the courtyard behind the Bold Arms.

Meols Hall. The entrance gates to the Hall are almost opposite St Cuthbert's Church. When the two families came together through marriage, the village pubs changed their names to the manorial titles: the Bold Arms and the Hesketh Arms.

When you walk into the public bar of the Bold Arms (formerly the Griffin) you are in the room that was the ale-house of more than 300 years ago. The lounge was created by adding rooms from two old neighbouring cottages; the restaurant extension came some hundred years later. Evidence of the Bold family connection can be seen from the silver griffin on the fireplace and in a number of stained-glass panels in the bow windows at the rear of the pub.

It was landlord William Sutton who looked ahead. The row of stables in the courtyard is a reminder of the layout of pubs that were in the coaching business. Horses were tethered on the cobbles at the front; a wooden railing there is of historic interest too. It is clear that people came to Churchtown to visit, also possibly en route elsewhere and it was those who came in increasing numbers to enjoy sea bathing who appealed to his business sense.

They needed transport to the nearest and best bathing place: a beach 2 miles away at South Hawes. Since the only place where accommodation was available was at Churchtown, visitors were taken from there to South Hawes by horse and cart: profitable it is true, but there was more in the bathing business than that for Sutton. There was no shelter at South Hawes where people could change into bathing 'suits', so in 1792 Sutton built one: a pretty ramshackle affair by all accounts. But that was only a beginning, because in 1798 he opened a hotel there, later known as 'The Duke's Folly'. Sutton's friends concluded that a distant sea pool was the nearest port to South Hawes, hence the name Southport.

This development not only attracted holidaymakers, but also people who wanted to live near the sea and had enough money to build a genteel house in the area. Churchtown was too marshy, so the new development took place in and around what is now the resort of Southport. As this was all land owned by the lords of the manors, there were strict controls over building in order to maintain 'tone' and respectability. Southport as a town centre was itself carefully planned, focused on Lord Street.

It would be nice to have a happy ending and to be able to give Sutton a title such as the Churchtown millionaire, but he fell into debt and was committed to Lancaster debtors' prison. But even he would have been astonished to see the many thousands who now visit Southport every year by road or rail. One could say quite reasonably that Sutton was the founder of the town. It is ironic that his motivation was to take people to the sea and by the 1860s the sea was retreating further and further away. An enormous pier was built out to the high-tide point; the distance to the end justified a tramway to take people to it!

Southport was for others to build and for others to take Sutton's place as land-lords of the Bold Arms. The pub is now a long range of five separate, but linked rooms with many hidden corners. It has always been a local activity pub: the coffee lounge, for example, was at one time used by Churchtown's pigeon fanciers. Racing birds were taken from the pub and released for a flight home.

When you visit the Bold Arms remember the 'if only' phrase. Round the corner from the pub are the Botanic Gardens. But for Southport they would certainly not be there: 25 acres of colour and activity, with a fernery, arboretum, lake, a variety of water birds, an aviary and a collection of small pets. Two fine bowling greens and Sunday brass band concerts are popular features.

The gardens always do well in the Britain in Bloom competition: in July expect to see geraniums, begonias, marigolds and, of course, roses in abundance. There is no entry charge.

CLITHEROE: SWAN & ROYAL

M6 to J31, A59 east, then A671; or M66, A56, cross M65 at J8, then A671.

There is something fascinating about the names of the famous; blue plaques on walls tell us where they were born or lived. Some towns even have a blue plaque trail, recognising the important part that the buildings and people played in local history.

Taking their courage and imagination in both hands, some property owners point to a particular room and say that it is the very place where a celebrity came into the world, or departed it. All good business, of course.

Like a full car park, a list of famous visitors is a mark of a pub's success. The painted bunch of grapes hanging over the front of the Swan & Royal is an indicator of good wines on offer; it is also a reminder of the most ancient of signs going back to Roman times when a bunch of vine leaves hanging outside told everyone that the

One of the most ancient of inn signs: the bunch of grapes above the main entrance of the Swan & Royal.

Clitheroe Castle from the Swan & Royal.

building was a place of refreshment. Today, of course, it would usually be a traditional painted inn sign.

But, as they say, the Swan & Royal was 'not just a pretty face'; originally known as the White Swan, it was a coaching inn with extensive stables. The Blackburn–Skipton coach called here in 1806. Coaching inns such as the Swan had a reputation for fast service, as passengers on the stagecoaches only had time for refreshments while the horses were being changed. Modern alterations of the bar area are attractive, but spaciousness in coaching days was always helpful if passengers, newly arrived, clamoured for attention – just as weekend and market-day visitors do in the twenty-first century. Latterly known simply as the Swan, it added Royal to its name in 1851 when it became the local headquarters of the Royal Mail, which had a service to Gisburn.

Situated as it is just below Clitheroe Castle on Castle Street, the Swan & Royal was bound to see the world facing its doors and to be part of the town's history. The castle is said to be the second smallest in the country and its function was more administrative than military; the last siege was during the Civil War, after which it was 'slighted' to prevent its possible future use against Parliament.

Violence did flare up in the nineteenth century as protests by the cotton-workers against the introduction of machinery took to the streets. There were seventeen cotton mills in Clitheroe at one time, providing work for many people; had it not been for the cotton industry, the town would never have grown to the size it did. Matters came to a head in 1878 when a crowd of cotton-workers threatened violence; the Swan & Royal itself seemed likely to be attacked and George Easton, a town alderman and magistrate, read the proclamation laid down in the Riot Act. Although the pub was guarded by a detachment of the 11th Hussars, Easton's pronouncement from the steps of the Swan & Royal was an act of some courage in the face of missiles of all kinds. Fortunately, serious bloodshed was avoided, but sadly the Hussars lost their lives in the Zulu War only six weeks later. Bedroom 1 at the Swan & Royal is named the George Easton Room.

In earlier and more peaceful times the Swan was the preferred venue for meetings of the Corporation of Clitheroe and Governors of the Grammar School, as well as for social events such as hunt balls and concerts in its Assembly Room.

To the right of the bar a series of framed photographs in the lounge area recalls the day in November 1942 when a deal was struck that would eventually transform air travel. Sir Frank Whittle, who invented the jet engine, was originally based in Coventry; the factory where he carried out his research was bombed in 1941, after which he relocated to Clitheroe, where his project was successful. The deal in 1942 transferred responsibility for Whittle's invention from the Rover Car Company to Rolls-Royce. It was sealed over a 5-shilling meal! Sir Frank used the Swan & Royal regularly to dine and to hold conferences. Bedroom 4 is named the Sir Frank Whittle Room; in his honour it has a four-poster bed and a fine view of the castle.

It is not surprising that the Prime Minister of the time, Winston Churchill, wanted to be kept informed of progress of the jet engine project and stayed at the Swan and Royal several times. Bedroom 2, a large room at the front has been named the Sir Winston Churchill Room; there is also the Sir Winston Churchill function room, which can accommodate up to 100 people and has its own bar and stage.

Room 3 has an even more unusual dedication: the Gandhi Room. He stayed at the Swan & Royal in 1933 when he came to visit a cotton mill at Low Moor. He was so impressed that he took ideas back to India to help him to develop cotton manufacturing there.

When booking in at the Swan & Royal you can justifiably feel that you are joining the ranks of the famous, and the Ribble Valley will delight you. The tourist information centre and the library stand close together just below the pub at the bottom of Castle Street. Visit them both.

The plaque 'Pioneers of the Jet Engine' and the photographs recall Sir Frank Whittle's visits to the Swan & Royal and his work at Clitheroe developing the jet engine.

CONDER GREEN: *THE STORK*

M6/A6 to Lancaster. Continue to south of city centre. At roundabout take A588 signed Glasson. Pass Golf Club. A sharp, unexpected bend turns right to Conder Green. Watch for facing traffic approaching Stork car park round second sharp bend.

The river Lune is out of sight but never out of mind. The water's edge is close enough for floods to be an ever-present risk, and the land is flat and featureless. Stretching out from the Stork car park and from the track that passes the front of the pub is a sea of tall, waving grass and rushes. Beyond the arched bridge over the little river Conder traffic can be seen moving along the road to Glasson Dock. Here and there deep in the grass are abandoned clumps of yellow flag iris or of brightly coloured 'red hot pokers'; otherwise all is green.

The Stork stands out sharp and white on the bend of the road (dangerous here!), with its wrought-iron bird over the door, black and aggressive, red wings out-stretched. The pub has a place in history, having stood here for some 350 years, during which time it has had several changes of name, including that of The Cocks, thought to be a reference to the sport of cock fighting, once popular. In more recent times it was known as the Duke Hamilton Arms; the family were lords of the manor and their former home, Ashton Hall, is now part of Lancaster Golf Club, a mile along the road to Lancaster. The stork symbol from which the present name comes is on the crest of the Starkie family, who bought the Ashton estate after the Hamiltons.

It is quite easy to imagine the Stork in its early days with its narrow, steep stairs just inside the entrance and the inviting, tiny snug to the right, perfect for anyone to

The Stork at Conder Green stands looking out over the marsh towards the river Lune.

sit and write first impressions of the pub. Next to it is the games room, then the bar area, all regularly thronged with Stork visitors. In the bar area is a menacing-looking artillery piece that once stood outside; in a glass case is a fine metal stork on what seems to be a shoreline covered with pebbles.

An old painting in the bar shows a shop on the right-hand corner of the pub (selling sweets and 'goodies') and a barn at the other end, so it was a farm, too. The barn was added to the pub in recent years and is now a comfortable and spacious restaurant. At one time food was served on the upper floor.

A record of past licensees is kept in the bar: Christopher Caton is the first on the plaque, from 1660 to 1663, followed, of course, by a long list of others. The most recent entry is that of Audrey Margaret Brogden, 2002 to 2004.

Standing guard over the main door is a menacing stork, wings outstretched.

With no shop now at Conder Green (other than a farm shop), local people must be grateful for a bus stop at the Stork on the Lancaster to Fleetwood route. When there were thatched cottages opposite there would have been a visible community to be served, but those have now gone. Today you need to walk along the track in front of the pub to see most of the dwellings of Conder Green: a farm, bungalows, houses and cottages scattered along for about half a mile. After an evening meal it is wonderful to walk along, admiring gardens and enjoying the peace and quiet. In about ten minutes the track rises to the bridge that once carried the picturesque branch railway line from Lancaster to Glasson, now, sadly, gone, but the disused track bed remains as a fascinating route for walkers to Glasson. Bird watchers should take their cameras because of the number and variety of birds on the marsh.

Glasson is well worth a visit whether you walk along the railway track or drive from the Stork across the road bridge and turn on to the B6290. Almost 220 years ago, when shipping was experiencing silting problems on the river Lune, making it difficult to reach Lancaster, it seemed a good idea to build a wet dock at Glasson where freighters could berth, load and unload; a link with the Lancaster Canal was also completed. Although movement of freight by rail reduced the importance of Glasson, it is now more attactive than ever and visitors go there in large numbers. Some small merchant ships still go to the dock basin there and something of interest is always going on. The large canal basin is now a busy marina, with many cruisers and other leisure craft.

The Chapter House at Cockersand Abbey.

A visit of a very different kind, particularly for those with an interest in things historical, is to Cockersand Abbey. From the Stork take the A588 that passes the pub, cross the bridge and continue to Lower Thurnham. Turn towards the shore along Moss Lane signed Cockerham Sands Country Park. The narrow lane constantly winds, so watch for a gateway and sign that says Cockersand Abbey Farm. Leave the car parked safely and take the public right of way to the farm, which is close to the shore. Beyond the farm are the remains of the abbey, including the Chapter House, kept locked, as it was a burial place for the landowners, the Dalton family. The abbey was once no more than a hermitage, converted by the White Monks of the Premonstratensian Order into an abbey in 1190, becoming one of the wealthiest in the north-west.

There is an information notice at the impressive Chapter House, but the rest of the abbey consists of ruined pillars and outlines of walls. It is a very lonely and evocative place, just the sort of location a religious order would seek for a contemplative life. The views across the water are fantastic: Sunderland Point is quite visible (see the Overton Globe, pp. 118–21) and a lighthouse stands in solitude just to the north of the abbey site.

CROSTON: *THE LORD NELSON*

M61 to J8 (Chorley), then A6 south. Immediately turn right on A585 to Southport. Continue to A581 into Croston; look for village green beyond church and bridge.
Rail service from Preston.

The year 2005 was the anniversary of the Battle of Trafalgar and of the pub's name, having become the Lord Nelson after the great naval victory in 1805. So there was no better date to be at Croston than in time for all the celebrations planned for 21–23 October at and around the Lord Nelson: fireworks, Morris dancers and live music. Unmissable!

Old photographs of the pub show a flag pole and spar carrying flags with the famous message expecting every man to do his duty. This disappeared some time ago, but a new one was made in time for the October bicentenary: a happy ending.

Until 1805 the pub's name was the Green Man, not uncommon in the country as a whole and sometimes connected with Robin Hood, but much more likely a name going back to our distant past. The Green Man of legend was a god-like image of fertility, often a part played at early May Day celebrations by some local actor who was traditionally garlanded with green leaves. The Lord Nelson must have sounded more patriotic and uplifting in 1805.

At one time there were fourteen pubs in Croston; they are now reduced to just six – and over a period when the population has been increasing fast. It can only mean that selling ale or beer at Croston was for long a 'second-income' occupation, with the brew a domestic product sold from a building that was primarily a farm, or even a smithy. The Lord Nelson was originally a farmhouse, going back to the seventeenth century on the evidence of the thick walls, beams and flagged floors. Today's bar might well have been the farm kitchen, and the dining room, the family parlour and the smaller rooms at the front and back other domestic areas. The landlady believes that the brick outbuilding in the car park at the rear of the pub was originally a cowshed.

In the bar area there is a welcoming fire, and an old range in the dining room. Nelson's spirit is everywhere: large illustrations of *Victory* face the bar, and the windows look out on to the village green and the flag mast. Notices posted liberally on windows say 'We won' – not at Trafalgar, but at the Best Kept Village competition.

Unusually not a roadside pub, the Lord Nelson stands back modestly behind the village green at Croston. Look for it.

The Lord Nelson's immaculate bar and welcoming landlady.

Of the six remaining pubs in Croston, the Lord Nelson is the least conspicuous, as it stands back from the main street behind the village green, which is on the right as visitors enter the village from the Chorley direction. It is beyond the church of St Michael and All Angels and the famous packhorse bridge of 1682 over the river Yarrow. And yes – cars can still use the bridge, so do not be surprised as you turn the bend there to see a car bearing down on you from its high arch.

There is a patrons' car park at the Lord Nelson and public parking places behind the pub; whichever you use, walk back to the bridge and the cobbled Church Street because there the long history of the village is revealed. Its name almost certainly means 'village with a cross' and there it is – still on its ancient Saxon base. The cross itself disappeared over the centuries, as many did, and was replaced by a modern one; it was a preaching cross, used as a place of worship before the parish church was built.

Croston has always depended on agriculture and was an important centre with a market charter dating back to the thirteenth century. Flax was widely grown on the rich low-lying Croston Moss, and cottages once occupied by flax handloom weavers can be seen on Drinkhouse Lane on the edge of the village.

A glimpse of history: Croston Church Street with the Saxon stones forming the base of the cross. Close to the church (its tower 'leans') is the steeply arched packhorse bridge.

The Lord Nelson takes part in all local events, especially the annual traditions, such as Coffee Day in July. The name is derived from the old Feoffee Day, on which tenants came to pay their rents to the lord of the manor. Feoffees today are usually trustees who act as landlords of village properties on behalf of the community. Croston makes merry on Coffee Day, the pubs open their doors, so the first Saturday in July is a wonderful day to visit the village and, of course, the Lord Nelson, where there is a special barbecue.

For those who want to come back to Croston, and many will, Ruffold Old Hall is only twenty minutes away and Astley Hall near Chorley takes little more than that. Both are historically fascinating and visually two of the most spectacular houses in Lancashire.

DIGGLE, SADDLEWORTH
THE *DIGGLE HOTEL (Station House)*

A62 from Manchester or Huddersfield to Delph. At Delph, take A6052 to join A670 Standedge road. At Diggle sign take Huddersfield road through village. Pass church, turn at 'weak bridge'; pass primary school, cross bridge to pub.

There are times when many motorists are ready to throw up their hands in despair at the unhelpfulness of road signs. So it is when looking for the Diggle Hotel: road directions are given above, but having followed them into Diggle your problems may have only just begun. Driving cautiously through the village, you will

Diggle Hotel from the forecourt, venue for the Sunday afternoon brass band concerts.

notice signs saying 'Emergency vehicles' and 'Weak bridge', neither of which is very encouraging when you are searching for the Diggle Hotel.

Be brave! Ignore the weak bridge sign – it probably does not apply to you unless you have a tractor and a loaded trailer. Pass the primary school, go over the weak bridge and there you are. Eat under the trees that surround the cobbled forecourt, or take a table inside, but get there early as there are many people 'in the know' who find their way regularly and easily to this ancient pub. Food orders stop at 2.30 p.m., so allow plenty of time, especially if your planned route is via Delph, as road closures seem to happen there from time to time.

Certainly the Diggle regulars know what to expect. One journalist's record of a visit says it all: 'If you want a steak pie with a puff pastry top as light as an angel's wing, go to Diggle. The meat is tender, there's a lot of it – the pastry topping nearly floats off into the air.' Extravagantly put, but that's how it is and with plenty of alternatives on the menu, also a traditional lunch on Sundays, the Diggle Hotel enjoys a great reputation locally.

Music with a meal is always popular, and at the Diggle Hotel there is a quite unusual programme of band concerts on the forecourt on Sundays from May to September from 2 p.m. to 4 p.m. which they call 'The Best in Brass'. Saddleworth is big in brass, and prize-winning bands from the district figure largely in the programme.

In 2006 there will be even more interest and excitement with the First Diggle Brass Band Contest on 1 July. In Saddleworth they know a fine band when they hear

The western portal of the Standedge Tunnel of the Huddersfield Canal. Behind is the wild moorland through which the canal and railway tunnels were cut.

one, so the competition to be the winner on that first occasion will raise plenty of passion and a lively thirst: fortunately the pub is in the *Good Beer Guide*.

Luckily for the historian, records of the Diggle property have been preserved and show how the Broadbent family farmed here for generations. From the late 1500s the Ramsdens were landowners in Saddleworth, including Diggle. The earliest Broadbent land entry for Diggle Farm is that of a John Broadbent, who paid three shillings and seven pence to William Ramsden in 1590/91.

Most of the family smallholdings in Scammonden and district were freehold, but it appears that the Broadbents had their own rental system for ale-houses, which provided for a yearly rent to be paid to the main family home at Golcar. Quite remarkable is a copy of a history of the Diggle Farm Inn 1525–2002, showing all the Broadbent family names. There is little doubt that farming was the major occupation, but that the farmhouse also served as an ale-house; an indenture of 1637 refers to the Diggle Inn. Other references in early trade directories of Saddleworth give it the name Diggle Farm Inn. A photograph of a Broadbent family gathering is dated 1911.

Today's Diggle Hotel has a bar area that spans the whole building, with two additional small rooms set out with tables and chairs, one to the front and one to the rear. Both would have been separate rooms at one time before internal alterations were made; a commemorative wall-display plate dates the hotel officially as it was produced for its centenary and dated 1789–1989.

It may seem a little odd that the other plates on display – Denby Dale Pie 1964 and Hebden Bridge Dock Pudding with recipe – are Yorkshire commemoratives. This is entirely because the fourteen villages including Diggle in the parish of Saddleworth were in Yorkshire until 1974; now they are part of the Metropolitan Borough of Oldham. A fine colour photograph of Rush Bearing and the Saddleworth Morris Men hangs in pride of place.

Even if the Diggle Hotel had not claimed space in this book on account of its age and its place as a focal point of the hamlet of 'Diglea', it would have justified entry because very close to the pub are the western portals (both canal and railway) of the Standedge Tunnel of the Huddersfield Canal, 5,686 yards long.

This was built in 1793 when 'canal mania' was at its height and is a great monument to the men who planned it and to the many who worked on it. Go out of the Diggle Hotel and turn right over the bridge; the road bears left and at the next turning is a telephone box marking the entrance to a shady car park. Over the wall is the canal tunnel portal, unbelievably only 7 feet wide, as the tunnel had no towpath and the narrow boats had to be 'legged' through. It was more than 3 miles and took about four hours, before reaching daylight again at Marsden in Yorkshire (see Marsden Tunnel End Inn in *Yorkshire's Historic Pubs* by Peter Thomas, Sutton). The rail track from Huddersfield and Marsden to Stalybridge and Manchester runs alongside the canal and passes through its own tunnel. There is a towpath walk along the open canal; it is full of interest, definitely a place to have a camera at the ready.

Whether or not your route to and from Diggle follows the A62 through Marsden, the drive to the Standedge Visitor Centre and the National Trust Estate Office near Marsden Station is fascinating. The overwhelming scale of the task faced by the tunnel builders and the determination they must have had to complete it can only be understood by driving over the hills between Diggle and Marsden. The country is wild: the only evidence of what lies below is the ventilation shafts.

DOBCROSS, NEAR OLDHAM
THE SWAN INN (or Top House)

*M62 to J21, A640 Denshaw, then A6052 Delph and Dobcross. A62
Manchester, Oldham, Delph, turn right, A6052 to Dobcross.*

In 1974 the people of Dobcross learned that they no longer lived in Yorkshire, but were now part of Greater Manchester. That did not make them Lancastrians, far from it, but as a result the Swan qualifies for inclusion in this book. It is worth noting that the excellent *Saddleworth Villages*, which includes Dobcross and was published by the Saddleworth Historical Society in 2003, gives the Society's address as 'Saddleworth, Yorkshire, England'.

Standing in the very centre of the village, in the Square, the Swan commands attention and observes all the goings-on. Built as a pub, rather than a conversion from a farmhouse, or from cottages, it has a datestone over the door showing 1765

So typical of the Saddleworth villages; the style of the Swan at Dobcross seen from the Square is unmistakable.

and the initials of Benjamin and Sarah Wrigley. This is a copy of the original stone and may be in error, as there is evidence of a pub here earlier than 1765, called the George.

Today's traffic comes to a halt regularly outside the Swan, especially when a bus arrives, so there is no room for a roadside telephone box, which sits on the pub's forecourt above street level, a bizarre arrangement when the building's age is taken into account. As if to emphasise the past, the glass in the main entrance door is engraved 'Kings Head'; immediately above is the present Swan wall sign, with a white swan hanging sign above the Square.

The inn's datestone.

Adjoining the Swan and to the left of the entrance is a house that 100 years after the pub opened was added to it; its ground floor has become the kitchen. Outside in the Square is a flower-decorated memorial to Dr Walter Henry Fox Ramsden, much-loved village doctor who began practising here in 1864. He died in 1900.

If it is a pedigree you seek, it can be seen in the bar, both the Wrigley will and the original indenture for the purchase of the property; the skill of the calligrapher is quite extraordinary. From the bar area three dining rooms open out, two on the front and one on the back, seating up to eighty people; by 1 p.m. on a February Thursday a free table was hard to find. Needless to say, good open fires provide a warm welcome.

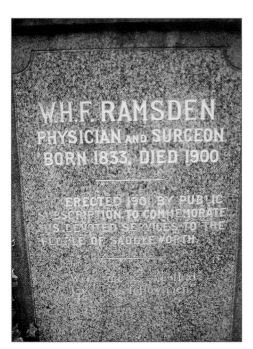

The memorial to Dr Ramsden.

As has always been the custom, the pub served the community in various ways: auctions would take place and meetings of societies were held. In the nineteenth century court cases were held upstairs in what is still known as the Court Room. Prisoners were held in the cellars pending their trial. Today the Court Room is used for booked lunches, such as those for Rotary.

It was in the nineteenth century too that changes of ownership or tenancy of a pub often brought bewildering changes of name. We have already seen evidence in the door of the change from Kings Head to Swan; a variation made it the Swan with Two Necks. As if anxious to exploit all its connections, the pub traded for a while under both names: Swan with Two Necks and the Kings Head. It eventually reverted to the Swan, but even then the Kings Head returned for a while as if the owner was reluctant to abandon the name altogether.

It is generally believed that where we were born and raised made us the sort of people we are. If proof were needed, you will find it in the Saddleworth district at Whitsuntide, when traditionally the churches have had their Whit Walks. Michael and Peter Fox in *A Saddleworth Whitsuntide* quote the memories of Ammon Wrigley, the Saddleworth author. He recalls the bands playing and the children in procession. He remembers: Old Esther o'th' Sheepcotes comes up and says, 'It would never be Wissen if aw didn't see th' children walk.'

By 1871 all the village Sunday schools had brought their various anniversary dates together and celebrations took place throughout the Saddleworth area on Whit Friday. This has created the tradition – more a way of life – involving the brass bands in an even greater part of the day's activities.

At Dobcross these begin with a short service in the Square led by the vicar from a raised area outside the Swan. Music for the hymns is provided by the Dobcross Band, which afterwards heads the procession into Uppermill, where the other village bands take part in a united service on the playing field.

In the afternoon there are games and sports; meanwhile, the bandsmen, having returned to their home villages (and the pubs for refreshment), rest and prepare for the evening band contest. This is a unique event – or series of events – as each band has ten minutes to play a piece of their choice in front of the judge before racing off to perform before judges at other Saddleworth villages. The aim is to play as many times as possible between 5 p.m. and 11 p.m. – as much a matter of luck as of organisation in avoiding a queue of bands waiting their turn to play. Each band plays last in its own home village; like all the other rules, it has always been so.

Competition is fierce, prizes are numerous, but village pride is the spur. Brass bands from all over Lancashire and Yorkshire compete, as well as from distant parts; when one of the Saddleworth village bands defeats a famous national band the achievement is recorded in local history and talked about for years.

DOWNHAM: *THE ASSHETON ARMS*

M6/M61 to J31, then A59; or M60 to J18, then M66, A56, cross M65 at J18, then A671/59.
Note: *In either case fork left on A59 for Chatburn – then turn right in village.*

A worthy contender for the title of a perfect village, Downham consists of two tiny groups of buildings: one at the foot of the hill by the village green, Downham beck and bridge, and the other that includes the pub, the church and cottages at the top. Here also is Downham Hall, the home of the Assheton family who bought the manor of Downham in 1558, the year that Elizabeth I came to the throne of England. Even earlier, as far back as the eighth or ninth century, there was a settlement here; written records exist of a medieval village in 1400.

The Assheton Arms.

Ralph Assheton received the title of Lord Clitheroe in 1956 and it was in recognition of the honour that the pub's name was changed from the George and Dragon to take the name of the family. Downham has been an estate village ever since the Asshetons became lords of the manor and their caring hand can be seen everywhere. It is unspoilt and uncluttered with TV aerials, modern signs and street furniture; truly the Asshetons have retained the best of the past. Jessica Lofthouse chose her words wonderfully well: 'Age-old antiquity, settled peace and architectural beauty.'

The pub is so right – in a position opposite the church – and grouped with handloom weavers' cottages nearby. Seats outside on the pub front are always popular in warm weather. With a view down the village street and across to Pendle Hill, the church in the trees opposite and Downham Hall beyond, who could ask for more?

Beamed within, the pub has just one bar facing the door; on the left is an old stone fireplace and beyond is a second dining area. On the right the furniture consists of tables and settles, giving comfort, warmth and privacy.

The Sunday night TV series *Born and Bred* was filmed at Downham, which was called Ormston in the programme; the pub became the Signalman's Arms. The award-winning film *Whistle down the Wind*, starring Hayley Mills when a young girl, was made in the area; a number of shots of the village street were used for background effect.

The Assheton Arms has the popularity of the village to thank for much of its business, especially at holiday times. More cosmopolitan than ever, the visitors seek a growing variety of menu dishes as well as the old faithfuls. The bottom line of the specials board said it all one day in 2005: 'Lancashire Hot Pot with mushy peas/Thai Green Chicken Curry'.

St Leonard's Church, Downham, with its fifteenth-century tower.

St Leonard's window with his prisoner's chain over his left arm.

As part of its service to the Downham community, the pub has for many years had so-called Rent Days when the local tenant farmers do business with their landlord and are given lunch. There is a post office in the village and a bus stops outside the Assheton Arms, but public services are limited to this.

St Leonard's Church should not be missed; the oldest part is the fifteenth-century tower. The remainder has been rebuilt twice, the last time in 1901–10. St Leonard was the patron saint of prisoners and cared especially for country people; a window depicting him is just inside the door, with a prisoner's chain attached. In the south-east corner of the church is the Assheton Chapel containing monuments to the family, with the vault below.

It is believed by some that three of the five bells in the tower are 'Monks' Bells' brought from Whalley Abbey, which was also in the ownership of the Asshetons. Old they certainly are and provide material for the story that they can be heard sometimes chiming softly on calm nights. However, it is more likely that they have been in the tower since it was built.

As you leave the church, stop and look at the view of Pendle Hill; Queen Mary visited the church in 1938 and thought it the most beautiful view from any church porch in the land.

But don't look for a signpost when you drive away – there isn't one. They are the kindest people here – just ask!

ENTWISTLE: *THE STRAWBURY DUCK*

By rail Bolton–Blackburn (hourly at most times). By road M61 to J3, then A6053 to Bolton, or M61 to J5, then A676 to Bolton. From Bolton A676 to Walves; at crossroads turn left to Edgworth; left at end of village. On Hob Lane cross Wayoh Reservoir to Entwistle.

If you know the West Pennine Moors, you will surely know of the Strawbury Duck; if not, you may well have a problem finding Entwistle listed in guide books or referred to by countryside authors as a Lancashire village. Small it may be, but it has its own railway station on the Bolton–Blackburn line; without it there would be no Strawbury Duck, as it was originally the Station Hotel. The train service was operating by 1848 and the pub began life around the turn of the century.

The nineteenth-century Station Hotel was much smaller than the present Strawbury Duck; in 1981 the former Bridge Cottage, some 300 years old and standing next door, was added to the pub. The story of how it acquired its odd name is an interesting one. For a long time it had been known locally as the 'Strawberry' from the colour of its stone walls in evening sunshine. In the 1970s a new owner decided to give its title a Lancashire town flavour, changing it to Strawbury and adding 'duck'

The black and white section of the Strawbury Duck is quite different from the original stone building on the right which reflected the evening sunshine and gave the pub its 'Strawberry' colour and name.

Food for walkers and fishermen is popular and although the bar is small there are plenty of tables for dining.

from his own name, Duxbury, hence Strawbury Duck. Like Hoover and HP Sauce the new name became an easily recognisable symbol. As if to make the change complete, the front of the pub was given a different colour scheme: black and white.

Apart from the station and pub there are few buildings to be seen other than a terrace of undistinguished cottages; visitors are therefore the life-blood of the Strawbury Duck. To photograph the front is a difficult enterprise as the deep railway cutting is only a few yards away, but it is worth persevering, particularly as a lovely clematis blooms in May close to the black-and-white section of the house.

The layout inside has rooms in all directions from the large L-shaped bar; leading off it to the left are two quite small rooms giving a feeling of intimacy. Behind the bar to the left and right are two further rooms that can seat fifteen or so diners and are regularly reserved for groups of walkers or bird watchers. Wherever one looks are prints of birds of all kinds on the walls; this is clearly outdoor country; fishing is popular, too (permits are required).

If you drive to the Strawbury Duck you will probably come from Edgworth, along Hob Lane (resurfacing is overdue here); the road passes across Wayoh Reservoir, a beauty spot in its own right and full of wildlife. The name Wayoh is said to come from Old English and to mean 'track along a ridge'. Completed in 1876, Wayoh Reservoir's purpose was to collect water for the growing mill town of Bolton, following the earlier opening of Turton and Entwistle Reservoir, also very close to the pub. As late as 1971 Jumbles Reservoir was opened further south; easily accessible from Bolton, its country park there is now a valuable leisure facility.

For those not wishing to venture far on foot there is a treasure nearby that does not require strenuous activity: Turton Tower, very close to Jumbles Country Park, off the A676 Bolton road. Once the manor house for a wide area, Turton Tower's oldest part is a stone 'pele', a more familiar sight on the English/Scottish border. Pele, or pole, is derived from a fence or stockade; towers of this kind were defensive. Under threat, people – and often their cattle as well – would retreat to the tower and its stockade for protection. Since the pele at Turton (hence Turton Tower) dates from the fifteenth century, life in the area must have been turbulent and dangerous at that time.

The original builders of the tower were the Orrell family; the rest of the house was built over 100 years later and its half-timbering shows how much more peaceful life had become. Turton Tower developed into a luxurious home, lavishly furnished with some of the most extensive decorative woodwork, painting and furniture in the region. Fabrics and wallcoverings include work by D.G. Rossetti and William Morris.

Although Turton Tower is neither tall, nor in a prominent hilltop position, conspicuous for many miles around is the Peel Tower, above the village of Holcombe, near Ramsbottom. Confusion with its name is not unusual.

It is not a pele tower, as the manor house at Turton was, although it may sound like it. It is a 128-foot stone monument to commemorate the life of Sir Robert Peel, successful industrialist and notable nineteenth-century prime minister, who was born at Bury. You may see it away to the east when travelling to and from Entwistle and the Strawbury Duck.

Turton Tower, built by the Orrell family, was primarily for defence – a mini-castle. The timbered house was added when times became more peaceful.

Lonely and austere, the Peel Tower's only welcome seems to be to those brave souls insisting on climbing up to it to be able to say 'the view was superb'. Fortunately, a successful pub like the Strawbury Duck offers much more, as its many regulars would agree with enthusiasm.

FOULRIDGE: *THE HOLE IN THE WALL*

M61 to J9, then M65 east to end (J14). Continue 1mile. A6068, turn left A56 (signed Skipton). Brown sign to Wharf and pub on left in village.
For Pendle Heritage Centre, Barrowford: M61/65 as above to J13. Turn left A682 (signed Kendal). Brown sign on right at end of Barrowford main street. Cross bridge, car park on left.

Standing at a village crossroads just 200 yards from the Leeds and Liverpool Canal is a pub with two signs and two (even three) separate businesses. The larger and usual painted sign shows the entrance to the canal tunnel, 1,640 yards long; the smaller, close to the tunnel sign and in total contrast, says 'Post Office'. A separate door, perhaps; but no, here is a quite unusual arrangement and nothing to do with the hole in the wall.

One theory about the pub's name follows the familiar line that at some time in the past drink was served through a small hatchery or hole in the wall to customers outside, perhaps because of congestion and difficulty of access. The landlord does not support this explanation, but favours the notion that whatever the pub's original

Today's Hole in the Wall showing its Post Office sign to the rear. To the left of the front door is the counter and food store.

name, the hole in the wall at the Foulridge, or north, end of the tunnel is the source of the present name. A careful look at the sign, of which he is very proud, shows not only the tunnel entrance, but the famous cow Buttercup in the canal.

Buttercup gained fame in 1912 when she fell into the water at the Barrowford end of the tunnel. For reasons known only to Buttercup, and she was never able to say why, she decided to swim the whole 1,640 yards to the Foulridge end, where she was rescued and revived by alcohol. As the Hole in the Wall sign says, 'Why not revive yourself?' Such was Buttercup's achievement and her fame afterwards that the pub placed a photograph of her in the bar with a brass plaque below it. An unlikely heroine, certainly, but worth her weight in gold for publicity.

The door with the bar parlour, now the Post Office.

Around the bar is a series of pictures of the pub as it was in the past – and it goes back a long way. A 'likeness' of 1780 shows it as very different from a 1909 photograph which portrays the Hole in the Wall after a rebuild in recognisably today's form. There were three public rooms, the main bar at the front, a games room at the back and on the left of the entrance what was formerly a small dining room. Too small to be really worthwhile, says the landlord, and on the cold side of the house.

When the village lost its post office and only general store the landlord decided to convert the small dining room (the bar parlour) into the post office. So when he is not pulling pints he can be seen selling stamps or working on his post office accounts. And that is not all: the displays below the post office counter include sugar, salt, bags of flour, tea and coffee. Such vital items as baked beans and HP Sauce are there too!

A housewife in Foulridge need never be desperate in her kitchen while there is a Hole in the Wall, and beer drinkers can rest in the knowledge that real ale will always be available.

Some 200 yards down Towngate from the pub is the Canal Wharf, where the former wharf office serves as a small museum; moored alongside is the *Marton Emperor*, operated by Foulridge Canal Cruises Ltd. On Sunday afternoons in the summer she departs for one-and-a-half-hour cruises to Salterforth; on the last Sunday in the month there is a two hour trip through the tunnel to Barrowford Locks. Private charters are available and there is a small vessel for private hire.

Before the coming of the canal Foulridge was little more than a collection of hamlets, most of the employment being on farms with a second income from

The canal arch at Foulridge, just where Buttercup ended her famous swim in 1912.

handloom weaving. Once work on the canal began in 1790 life was never the same again. The wharf and warehouse were built in 1815 and by then most of the local employment was connected with the canal. Horses and stables had to be provided, but as there were no towpaths in the tunnel the boats had to be 'legged' through. It is said that skilled men could 'leg' a loaded barge through the tunnel in an hour. Many jobs were available that had not existed before the canal was opened.

It is a constant surprise, walking along the towpath towards Salterforth, or gazing from the deck of the *Marton Emperor*, to see the low-lying meadow-land called the Bottoms with the Pennines so close. Oddly enough, Foulridge represents the summit of the canal; on either side of the village and beyond the tunnel entrance are the supply reservoirs.

Because water is spent in operating canals, they need a regular source to 'top up' their levels and two reservoirs above Foulridge and another at Barrowford do so with water they take from hillside streams. If you stand at the Foulridge tunnel entrance there is a constant sound of rushing water.

Do not be misled into thinking that the village name refers to something unpleasant. It came from the Anglo Saxon 'fola' or 'foal': on that basis we can conclude that it represents a ridge where foals were grazed.

This is good walking and cycling country, with excellent guide material at the Pendle Heritage Centre at Barrowford very close by. That is the place to start a visit to Foulridge. Parking there by the bridge opposite the Heritage Centre is easy – and the Victoria sponge baked there is magic!

GARSTANG: *THE ROYAL OAK*

A6 from north or south, turn off at B6430. B6430 southbound becomes one-way entering High Street. At marketplace keep right at the Royal Oak. Pub car park is on the left.
Note: If you miss your turn, go on to the bridge, turn right and go round again via Park Hill Road and Croston Road.
Northbound on B6430 from A6 keep left at bridge and follow Park Hill Road and Croston Road, then High Street as above.

A market town, a marketplace and a pub run by several generations of the same family: a rare combination and one that creates something special. Thus it is at the Royal Oak where collecting the history of the pub from old records has been a labour of love for the family. Walk through the Royal Oak and count the number of old drawings and prints that show the pub and the marketplace in past days: one dining area has three within an arm's length.

One view shows the former Royal Oak as a coaching inn, another as a timbered building with a garden across the front and a railing, yet another as a twenty-first-century pub and recognisable to anyone from Garstang. Looking out on to the activities of the marketplace and to the business of the street market, the Royal Oak is intimately involved with the life of the town. That importance is emphasised by the town's market cross outside, erected in 1754, although Elizabeth I granted royal permission for a market much earlier, in 1597. The 'cross', really a column topped by a ball, was restored as part of the celebrations to mark Queen Victoria's jubilee in 1897.

The Royal Oak is the kind of place where local people of any age can feel comfortable to eat and drink, and visitors to stay. Its furniture and furnishings are

The handsome front of the Royal Oak, facing the market cross. Keep to the right of the cross for the pub car park. The High Street is southbound only.

The stairs and half-landing at the Royal Oak.

tasteful and kept spotless; a linked series of small dining areas stretches across the front of the pub with a large dining and breakfast room at the end furthest from the bar. On the corner by the bar is an oak-panelled room looking much as it has been for many years, and is very popular with the regulars. One of the pleasures of a resident at the Royal Oak is the use of the handsome stairs with a half-landing furnished with good antiques including a grandfather clock. The bedrooms are large, and modernised in the same good taste as the rest of the house.

The Royal Oak is believed to have been a pub as far back as the fifteenth century. Originally part of the Garstang Manor Estate, it was sold by auction in November 1919 when the estate was broken up; as Lot 3 it was described as having stables and grassland.

Many alterations have taken place over the years, in the course of which a large well was found in the cellar; it was capped and is thought to have some connection with an old brook that once ran down the side of the Royal Oak to the river Wyre. Two levels were discovered in the old stables, the upper probably for storage of hay and the accommodation of stable-boys; a sink was found in the corner. When the pub had major work done in 1992 ancient walls of wattle and daub, and plaster and horsehair, were uncovered. The timbered outside walls had been removed earlier because the ground-floor timbers had rotted away; moisture from the front garden was blamed for this.

Violence came to Garstang during the Civil War, not least because Greenhalgh Castle, built in 1490 by the Earl of Derby, held out for the King; it was one of the last two garrisons in Lancashire to resist Parliament. Only part of one tower remains today and there is no public access.

War came again with the rebellions of 1715 and 1745, and spies were everywhere; one was staying at the Royal Oak. A sort of Home Guard was formed to keep watch and deny supplies to the rebels.

The Royal Oak landlords are listed in the pub records since 1807, but these are fragmentary earlier than that date. In 1890 there were 'Eight beds for travellers'; refreshment other than drinks could be provided for 110 persons, stabling for twelve horses. Then there were sixteen pubs in Garstang: today four exist, but for how long?

There were some notorious landlords and landladies (guests too!); coach passengers enjoyed Mary Proctor's hospitality, but a later landlord, James McKie, failed to satisfy Sir Walter Scott. He slept at the Royal Oak in 1828 and called it 'an indifferent house'. Fortunately, the novelist William Black thought otherwise when he stayed at the pub in 1875; he wrote, 'I give you my word this is the best ale we have drunk since we started from London; it is clear, bright, very bitter, brisk, it is worth the long journey to drink such ale.'

More recently, the visitors' book has an entry for 19 July 1904 by Dr and Mrs Ballantyne and their party from Glasgow: 'Delighted with the excellent luncheon and attendance. It reminds me of the good old times.' At one time Trevor Howard and Helen Cherry often visited the Royal Oak for a meal and a drink.

The Royal Oak is a fine representative of a fine town; June and July in particular have masses of colour everywhere, at road junctions and in the garden opposite the tourist information centre at the entrance to the car park. The town has won several awards in the Britain in Bloom competition; it has the unique title of the World's

The splendid aqueduct on the outskirts of Garstang designed by John Rennie carries the Lancaster Canal over the river Wyre.

First Fair Trade town, supporting an Oxfam-led initiative to fight global trading inequalities. If you can choose when you visit Garstang, market day is on Thursday and is not to be missed.

Further afield, Lancaster and Preston are both only 12 miles away, with a wide variety of visitor attractions. At Lancaster are the medieval castle, the beautiful Priory Church and Williamson Park with its Ashton Memorial; Preston's Harris Museum and Art Gallery, and the Museum of Lancashire attract thousands of visitors. Preston market is an institution in its own right.

GOOSNARGH: *THE GRAPES*

M6 to J32, turn on to M55. At J1 take A6 north to Broughton. Take B5269 Whittingham Lane, signed Longridge. Opposite Whittingham Post Office turn down Church Lane to pub and church.

Everything you would expect to see at an ancient village crossroads is there: church, school, manor house, village green and pub (in fact two pubs). And what a curious name the village has! As in neighbouring Grimsargh, Norse in origin, 'argh' is thought to be a field, or a piece of cultivated land. The first part of the name is more open to speculation; in the case of Goosnargh an Irish connection is possible

The pub's name and the vine painted behind it are a reminder of the very earliest signs for a drinking house.

The figures on the wall at the Grapes are above the 'Ode to an inebriate'.

and some suggest that the whole name simply means 'Goosefield'. Grimsargh looks more completely Norse, with 'Grim' possibly being a family name.

The Grapes has an interesting history too. Built as a pub, its earlier name was the Saracen's Head, a symbol used in heraldry by great families whose men joined in the Crusades; it was used later on pub signs. Over the centuries it seems to have begun to portray the courage of Saracen fighters. A change of name at Goosnargh took place following the occupation of the village in the Civil War by Cromwell, who is said to have used the pub and named it from one of his commanders, General Elliot. The pub's age can be measured in several hundreds of years, and one story has a fifteenth-century priest at the parish church licensee of the pub as well!

In addition to a games room to the left of the bar, there are two main dining areas at the front of the pub that have been opened up to provide more space; a smaller snug at the back completes the public accommodation. The reputation of the Grapes for food brings regulars from distant villages, no doubt as a result of its inclusion in both the *Good Pub Guide* and the *Good Beer Guide*. It has also been awarded a Pub of the Season accolade.

A feature of particular interest in the bar is a wooden wall exhibit made for the Fox and Grapes at Preston, entitled 'Ode to an inebriate'. Under a group of figures are the following lines:

Not drunk is he
who from the floor
can rise alone to
still drink more

But drunk is he
who prostrate lies
without the power
to drink or rise

Not just one pediment, but two, on the façade of Bushell House. Said to have been built in 1735, the rainheads clearly show 1722!

The lords of the manor here were the Bushells; just across Church Lane from the pub is the impressive Georgian Bushell House. In the eighteenth century William Bushell gave his elegant home to be used as a 'hospital', or residential home for elderly Protestant folk.

A short walk would take you to what is alleged to be the most haunted house in the country: Chingle Hall, built by the Singleton family in 1260. Return from the pub in the centre of the village to the B5269 Broughton to Longridge road and turn west towards Broughton; at the end of the village the entry to a metalled private road is alongside a public footpath sign. Take the footpath, which immediately joins the road; half a mile along, the road passes a bungalow, then a farm. Just beyond on the right is the white-walled Hall, once surrounded by a moat, traces of which can be seen, also the brick-walled bridge or passage that crossed it.

The much-haunted Chingle Hall. Father John Wall, executed for heresy, is said to be searching for his head, reputedly buried here.

Today Chingle Hall is no longer open to the public, but it is known to have been used for secret Roman Catholic worship when that was forbidden and there are a number of 'priest holes'. Restoration work has been going on in recent months apparently to deal with the effects of age; one wonders what may have been uncovered.

GREAT HARWOOD: *THE VICTORIA*

M65 to J7, then A6185 to the Business Park. Turn left, A678 to Rishton. At High Street lights turn right (Harwood Road). Keep right on A6535 into Blackburn Road. Pass cemetery on right, then Moss Street. At next right turn take St Hubert's Road. At church turn right into St John's Street. The Victoria is at the far end.

Built in 1905, 'the pub, not me', said the landlady. She came to the pub as she felt she needed a change of direction, and it has proved an inspired change for everyone concerned. She has never regretted it. She says her regulars are 'brilliant' and there is no doubt whatever that they think *she* is brilliant. Four years ago, when she arrived, it was they who helped her clean the place, and they seem as proud of it as she is.

Opened to serve the local railway, long gone, the pub's familiar name locally was 'Butcher Brig' because of the cattle brought to the slaughterhouse that stood in open land in the distance. The Victoria is at the bottom of St John's Street in Great Harwood; beyond the pub now are allotments, pigeon lofts and countryside. Great

The Victoria at Great Harwood looks like a railway inn.

Harwood ends here as if on a seashore; the garden has a large lawn with a fine view at the back (once a bowling green), and its walls and colourful flower beds make an attractive sitting-out area. This spacious garden and the wide front of the pub combine to present it as a comfortable Edwardian family home.

On a quiet evening the regulars congregate facing the end of the bar, which stretches across the area to the right of the entrance, with screens above and beer pumps on both sides. On busy evenings there are five (yes, five!) separate rooms, their names picked out on door panels of etched glass above twin panels with beautiful etched foliage patterns. The names above the doors no longer represent the current use of the rooms: 'Public Kitchen' is now a handsome games room with pool and darts, next to it, on the front, is the 'Commercial Room', which once must have been for business visitors. The 'Parlour' is a snug looking out on the garden; there are two intriguing notices near the bar on doors that might, once, have led outside. One says 'Smoke Room', the other, 'Jug Department' (there is neither an off-licence area, nor a taproom). These are, respectively, the gentlemen's and ladies' cloakrooms, and are a tribute to whoever planned the layout here.

Fascinating as all this may be, it is the outstanding quality of the interior of the Victoria that commands attention and has brought a CAMRA award and a listing (one of two in Lancashire) in the CAMRA National Inventory. The entry is but a brief summary: 'Edwardian railway pub with richly varied decor: superb tiling: counter screens: five rooms.'

If you enjoy art nouveau decoration, here you have it in abundance. It is a form of design that sprang from the Arts and Crafts Movement and is epitomised by its vigorous and elongated patterns using natural forms in a whole variety of media. At the Victoria the quantity and beauty of the etched glass is remarkable – and fortunately it has survived intact for almost a hundred years. The glazed tiling is even more spectacular: taken to full wall height, the cream-and-green art nouveau patterns are of the highest quality. To see their full beauty, go to the rear of the bar, where they decorate the whole of the walls to the upper floor. A unique experience!

A sample of the Victoria's stained glass panels (the Jug Department).

How could they have reached 2005 undamaged? A very careful examination reveals small marks locating fixing points for a covering. At some time in the past this treasure was boarded over; before reacting critically to such a 'sin', we should remember that the result is their survival and should be eternally thankful for that. The panelled ceilings remain, as do a large collection of photographs showing the Victoria in the past. Even royalty used the railway whose passengers the Victoria served; one wonders if they swept past, or perhaps called in.

The bar at the Victoria with some of its many green and cream Art Nouveau patterned tiles.

It is no surprise that the Victoria is a Grade II listed building. For visitors who appreciate the quality of the drinks there as well, it is in the *Good Beer Guide*. This pub has been described as a 'gem': pay a visit and meet the landlady – she is a gem, too.

But do not, whatever the temptation, give up the search for the Victoria on St John's Street, neither of which is easy to find. With the help of a friend at the bar, I now know the best route from the motorway avoiding Great Harwood town centre as given above. My friend uses it every day, knows her district and deserves a 'freebie', which she will receive from me on my next visit.

HASKAYNE: *THE SHIP INN*

From Liverpool, A59T to Maghull, fork left, A5147. From Preston, A59T through Ormskirk, then B5195. At Downholland Cross turn right, A5147. At Haskayne crossroads the Ship is just to the east.

First impressions are important: in the case of the Ship Inn words seemed inadequate. It was a warm, sunny day, the car park was full, and the pub empty, as everyone was sitting out on the canal bank. The rose garden was in full bloom and the white fence round it was immaculate. Coot with their young broods were circulating placidly round the tables on the grass, taking whatever food they could find back into the canal or some other place of safety to eat. All one can find to say is 'This is as good as it gets.'

On warm days the large centrally located bar takes the drinks and food orders; just a few steps further and visitors are on the grass by the canal where there are

The Ship Inn's rose garden is a colourful welcome on arrival in the pub car park.

plenty of tables and seats. The indoor dining areas face the canal bank and the waterborne activity; the eyes of diners outside turn regularly to the steeply arched road bridge over the canal at the corner of the pub garden. Most of the traffic under it is of water birds; there are three busy coot families always in residence and occasionally a brightly coloured narrowboat will pass under the arch.

Beyond the arch are permanent moorings on the former towpath. Grass verges now cover the cobbled tracks where horses used to pull boats loaded with coal and grain from the west; flour from local mills was an important outward cargo.

This is the Leeds and Liverpool Canal, at 127 miles the longest canal in Britain built by one company. It was authorised in 1770 and cutting began close by at Halsall; unexpectedly they found a stone ridge below the surface, useful for building stone, but a problem for a canal. It was found to stretch across the countryside, eventually reaching the north Wales coast. This meant changes of route, longer journeys for canal traffic and more lock gates. The Ship has been at Ship Bridge ever since there was a canal; it is claimed to be the first pub on the waterway.

Close to the houses below the bridge, where most of the permanent moorings are, you can see the huge block of stone beneath the level of the towpath which helped horses that fell into the water to find their footing out of the canal. Horses were changed here, so it was a busy bridge and a well-used pub.

The narrowboats here, which are permanently moored and lived-in homes, are surprisingly comfortable; every modern convenience is available. Passing down from the stern, bedroom, lounge, kitchen and bathroom are carpeted and furnished like any modern luxury home with sun decks fore and aft.

One of the Ship Inn's visitors: a coot searching for food.

Beyond the bridge are attractive homes: some, like *Cassandra*, are water-borne.

The end of a cruise: Frank assisting some of his disabled passengers.

Looking at these comfortable homes and at the costly cruisers moving up and down the canal, it would be easy to imagine that waterborne leisure activities are exclusively for the affluent. They certainly don't believe that at the Ship; a model in the bar of the *Pride of Sefton* is an important collecting box. The *Pride of Sefton* is a very special narrowboat and at 3.30 p.m. most days the cry goes up 'Frank is here!' Passing by the Ship, he will be taking his boat to its moorings just past the pub. He has been given a special parking area by the pub and a right of way to the towpath.

Since 1984 Frank has been in command of the *Pride of Sefton*, providing enjoyment of the waterways for thousands of disabled people in the region. The boat has a raised deck and large windows, so that even wheelchair users can enjoy cruising. There are comfortable cabin seats that can be converted into beds and all mod. cons are on board. Ramp access and a width of 11 feet make it possible to accommodate people regardless of their disability – even overnight.

Up to twelve passengers can be taken on cruises of whatever length requested, and the service is in great demand. Although in the early days it was supported by public funds, it is now dependent on sponsors, donations, appeals and collections such as that at the Ship. Charges now have to be made to cover running costs, but demand has never slackened.

It is unusual and unexpected to find a pub so closely associated with a social activity like the *Pride of Sefton*, and any visitor to the Ship would find it greatly inspiring to meet returning passengers and to talk to Frank. Ask at the bar where he has gone and his return time: if it has been a day trip, it is usually 3.30 p.m.

HEATON-WITH-OXCLIFFE
THE GOLDEN BALL, or *SNATCHEMS*

From Lancaster, A683 towards Morecambe. Continue A683 towards Heysham. Turn left at white sign for Overton. Turn left at brown sign for Golden Ball Inn. Follow shoreline.

A first impression of the Golden Ball is totally dependent on the weather and the state of the tide. It is said at the pub that the name Golden Ball came from the sun's glow as it rose over the Trough of Bowland and was reflected in the water of the river Lune just below the pub.

As to the danger of the tide, it has flooded the pub on a number of occasions in spite of its being raised up above the road; for proof look at the flood marker on the white wall along the bank beside the pub. It is higher than the top of your car, but you are not likely to decide to park your car there in any case; a Euroclamp notice warns you of the consequences if you park there without permission. You will go up the slope beyond the pub and park at the back out of the clamper's way.

Having explained 'Golden Ball', what about the curious 'Snatchems'? There has been a pub here since about 1650, the present building dating from the early 1700s, now listed and protected from alteration. As old as it is and standing almost alone for miles along the river bank, there are past happenings that explain the affectionate local name for the pub.

It is believed that, together with 'Catchems', downstream, the Golden Ball was popular with press gangs snatching men for service on warships. The name comes

Snatchems (or the Golden Ball), either name will do, seen from the riverside.

The tiny bar at the Golden Ball/Snatchems.

from 'prest', the payment of the monarch's shilling as an acceptance by a so-called volunteer of a binding contract to serve on board ship. The press gang would buy a local man a drink through some trickery or other; when he reached the bottom of his tankard he might well find the shilling there and be compelled to join a ship's crew bound for some unknown destination and uncertain fate.

As the locals began to realise their peril from the press gangs, tankards were made with glass bottoms so that the shilling could be seen and the offer of a drink refused. Eventually tankards became all glass; a selection of the original tankards is on display behind the bar.

By an odd coincidence yet another and similar name to Snatchems was in use for the district, which was known locally as 'Thatchems', through the custom of roofing houses with thatch. The river beds provided plenty of reeds for roofs and the pub was a meeting place for thatchers; a fragment of their work is still in the roof above the front of the bar.

Entering the pub from the rear car park, you will have the odd impression of going down into the cellar, since the back entrance and kitchen are at the 'top' of the house, with the bar downstairs at the lower entrance level. All the bar windows face the river, with huge views both up- and downstream; at this point the river is some 100 yards across, with sweeping, curved shores. It needs no imagination to understand how quickly the river might flood; there are spectacular photographs of floods on the walls near the front door.

A small area with padded benches and barrels for tables faces the tiny bar and there are larger rooms for dining and drinking at both ends of the building. You may wonder where the regulars live, in the absence of any community around the pub. Because it is not a village-based pub, they do, of course, come from a wide area and are joined by visitors attracted by the pub's name and reputation. Word gets around among the caravanners staying nearby that the food and drink at Snatchems is first class, and there are special facilities and menus for children.

Out on the patio is an information point (No. 3) set up as part of the river Lune Millennium Park. A large illustrated notice lists the bird life to look for and there is certainly plenty both on and out of the water.

All year round the river and salt marshes are home for greylag and Canada geese; in early spring they are joined by flocks of pink-footed geese on their way from their breeding grounds in Iceland. There are mute swans in large numbers, sometimes whooper swans from Iceland and Bewick's swans from Siberia.

Walkers and bird watchers will notice how some bird species like snipe and waders favour the pub side of the river for nesting. The meadows here are grazed by cattle, while those of the opposite side are grazed by sheep and attract the migrant pink-footed geese.

This area west of the Lune is like another world, although not far from Lancaster geographically. The further south the road goes, the more remote it gets and the river becomes even more fascinating.

HEST BANK: *HEST BANK HOTEL*

M6/A6 to Lancaster. Take A6 north. About one mile beyond the outskirts of Lancaster, fork left on to Hest Bank Lane. (There are two alternative turnings close by.)

Church towers have long since served as landmarks for travellers, some even with a guiding light for those who are overtaken by darkness and are lost in unfamiliar countryside; bomber crews during the Second World War looked for Lincoln Cathedral to help guide them back to their airfields in the eastern counties.

Rare it must be for a pub to serve the same guiding purpose: Hest Bank Hotel was that rarity through its position at the southern end of the route across the sands of Morecambe Bay to the Cartmel coast; in the coaching days it was the shortest (hardly a 'normal'!) way of reaching the Grange-over-Sands/Kents Bank district.

Such was the importance of the Hest Bank that its Lantern Room was built in 1799 to fulfil its purpose as a lighthouse. There have been many tragedies and rescues on the Oversands route: the tide comes in very swiftly, the sands are forever changing and some risk-taker or other will always try a crossing without the essential local knowledge.

The pub's early name was the Sands Inn, dating from at least 1554 when it was first licensed and had its own brewery. It may well have traded earlier, unlicensed, as it is known to have provided hospitality for travelling monks from religious houses such as Furness Abbey. These houses were closed in 1539/40 at the Dissolution of

The Hest Bank's front is on the roadside; its gardens at the rear are on the canal bank.

the Monasteries, so we are looking at a really early date for the pub's building; the use of cobbles at the rear as a building material confirms this.

History, it seems, could not leave the Hest Bank alone; both sides in the Civil War used and abused it until it was little more than a wreck. A hundred years later it was used by the soldiers who had marched with Bonnie Prince Charlie as far south as Derby before losing heart and the will to fight. With no booty or food, they made the Hest Bank a target as they returned north. Successive landlords must have felt that they were targets, too, yet in spite of the constant threat of highwaymen, the inn continued in business. If anyone expected, or even hoped for, quieter days, they were disappointed; in 1792 the innkeeper shot and wounded Edmund Crosse, a highwayman who was later convicted and hanged, his body being left on a nearby gibbet as a warning to others.

Then came the canal, the 'navvies' and the riots. But better days were coming at last for the Hest Bank with the growth of the coaching trade. It became an important posting and service stop, with extensive stabling and every comfort for travellers – even a rescue team. There were daily coach services across the sands with a fare of 7 shillings outside and 10 shillings inside; then came the railways, bringing to an end this adventurous journey. The last coach crossed in 1856. Fortunately the railways were to bring large numbers of visitors and open up Morecambe and Hest Bank as holiday resorts.

Seen in cold print, the location of the Hest Bank Hotel by the side of Bridge 118 of the Lancaster Canal may appear unimpressive, but the leafy approach from the A6, modern bungalows, retirement homes and large houses with extensive gardens all tell of a popular and affluent district. The Hest Bank, with its attractive canalside garden and its immediate surroundings including the canal bridge, are a combined delight. There is no parking problem.

The pub is a long building with a large dining area, both left and right of the bar, a non-smoking room facing the garden and another main lounge at the rear. The standard of the decor and the quality of the food fully justify the Hest Bank's Gold Award in 2001 as Tenanted Pub of the Year. In 2002 it was nominated in its Pub Industry Awards by the *Morning Advertiser* for its Pub Food Silver Award.

Even more noteworthy is a framed document under the logo of the Lancaster and Morecambe College's School of Hotel, Catering, Hairdressing and Beauty Therapy. This is a recognition of the dedication and hard work of Sue and John Hughes in developing, with the College, hospitality workers for the future and the award of an industry professorship to them in their capacity as Directors of Nearby Waterside Inns and proprietors of the Hest Bank Hotel.

The Hest Bank Hotel has a long list of notable people who stayed there in the nineteenth century, including Prince Frederick of Prussia, Lord Hamilton and the Duke of Devonshire. The well-loved comedian Eric Morecambe used to drink at the Hest Bank.

The pub is a very active place, not least because the Bay shoreline is only a matter of yards away and the canal is at the bottom of the garden. Leaflets in the bar

The *Waterbus* making its scheduled stop at the Hest Bank Hotel to pick up passengers for Lancaster. Refreshments on board add to the pleasure of the leisurely journey.

The lonely shoreline at Hest Bank and the dangerous route across the sands to the Cartmel coast.

advertise Bay Walks from Hest Bank at weekends to Grange-over-Sands, with return transport available. In July the Hest Bank does a team walk across to raise funds for St John's Hospice in Lancaster.

Much less energetic are steambus and waterbus trips operated by Budgie Bikes (tel. 01524 389410). There is a regular Waterbus timetable for a return service from Carnforth to Lancaster. This calls at the Hest Bank Hotel in each direction and includes the Lune Aqueduct with magnificent views up- and downstream.

HOGHTON, RILEY GREEN: *THE ROYAL OAK*

M65 to J3, then A675 signed Walton le Dale. From Bolton, A675 north.
From Preston, A675 south. From Blackburn A674/A6061.

'A little gem on the way to Hoghton Tower', wrote the journalist looking for a good opening. True in its way, no doubt, but it hardly does the Royal Oak justice. It is surely more than a bonus for country-house visitors. Why not 'After dining at the Royal Oak, take the opportunity to visit Hoghton Tower?'

Watched over by Hoghton Tower from its wooded hilltop site, the Royal Oak was until modern times part of the great Hoghton estate. An important part, too, as the main entry road to the house once ran past the pub, which marked the end of the estate where it met the highway at Riley Green. Today Green Lane follows the line of that entry road for 100 yards or so until it reaches a field gate. Here you may find a warning notice in April and May during lambing time, requesting that dogs be kept on a lead. Beside the gate is a stile, which allows walkers to continue. The views are outstanding: away to the left is the square tower of the parish church, while ahead on the hilltop is the Hoghton Tower Gatehouse. Next to it a clump of trees conceals Hoghton Tower itself.

The Royal Oak dates back to about 1620; originally a farm, it would have had living space and outbuildings close by on the areas now used as car parks. It is believed that it was converted to a pub in 1711; then, many of the villagers, handloom weavers or workers on the Hoghton estate would have been 'regulars'. Riley Green is still a small community, so today's patrons come by car, many a considerable distance. The landlord says 'Anywhere from Southport to the Lakes'.

The Royal Oak stands in an enviable position at the junction of the A674/A6061 and A675. If you use the M65 motorway and turn off at Junction 3, there are several destinations, of which Walton le Dale leads to Hoghton. As soon as you leave the roundabout the white Royal Oak shows up only a short distance away at about 'one o'clock' in direction. The road passes over the Leeds and Liverpool canal where a board says 'Boat Yard'. It is not now a boat-building site, more a marina with moorings and a restaurant. This is a particularly beautiful stretch of the canal with footpaths alongside from the bridge.

The Royal Oak's front is garlanded with flowers, its new sign disappointingly lacking the oak which, at Boscobel, hid the fugitive Charles II following the defeat of his army by Cromwell at Worcester in September 1651. Oak Apple Day, 29 May (the King's birthday), is still remembered to celebrate the event; in 2051 Royal Oak pubs will probably be serving free beer as they did in 1951, but that is a long time to wait. What is worth remembering is the number of pubs where Charles, on the run, was given food and drink during the six weeks of his pursuit after Worcester. Some landlords took the enormous risk of sheltering him, knowing who he was. The

Originally a farm, the Royal Oak became a stagecoach stop, serving coaches from Blackburn and Preston.

King's escape route did not include Riley Green, but the Royal Oak name is a popular one and is used by many English pubs having no connection with Charles II.

As well as repainting outside, a number of alterations have taken place inside, but the traditional atmosphere has been retained: oak beams, log fires, settles and cushions. All four dining areas are on the front of the house as if to allow people to watch for the arrival of the stagecoach. Outside is Blackburn Old Road and the Royal Oak served coaches from both Blackburn and Preston.

Mercifully there is no canned music or juke boxes at the Royal Oak. Neither would be in harmony with the atmosphere or the menu; this is traditionally English and certainly suits the majority of the pub's diners. Attractive starters from the printed menu include black pudding slices with wholegrain mustard dip; from the main course menu haddock in Royal Oak's beer batter is very appealing. There is an extensive specials board as well.

Now for the confession. On my first visit the challenge of a massive minced beef and onion pie meant denying myself my favourite sweet. Second time round I ordered jam roly-poly and custard first, to avoid missing it again. Five years between main course and dessert must be something of a record! It was certainly worth the wait and the Pub of the Season award by CAMRA in 2003 is well merited.

As for a visit to Hoghton Tower, the house is one of those that should be on everybody's 'do not miss' list. Dating from 1565 and built by Thomas Hoghton, it is a magnificent manor house with two courtyards entered through a huge gatehouse

The traditional dining area at the Royal Oak.

The view towards the gatehouse at Hoghton Tower.

flanked by two square towers. The family and state rooms are located in the upper courtyard; the original fireplaces survive and there are fine examples of panelling installed at later dates. The King's Hall, where visitors were received in audience by the King, and his Bedchamber are reminders of the occasion when James I stayed at Hoghton Tower.

It was in the Banqueting Hall on 17 August 1617 that James I, having been well fed, 'knighted' that day's joint of beef, creating the name 'Sir Loin', which is used to this day. The great size of the Banqueting Hall makes it an outstanding example of its age and type; there is a minstrels' gallery and the tables used in the famous Sir Loin incident are still on view.

Less famous, but possibly more important, is the Shakespeare connection. In the accounts of Shakespeare's life there are repeated references to the 'seven lost years' between 1585 and 1592; it is now increasingly believed that he went to Hoghton as a schoolmaster and theatrical player in that period. The Banqueting Hall is where the Hoghton players performed and there is a family tradition that Shakespeare worked for them for a time. It is an intriguing possibility that he trod the boards for the first time at Hoghton and that likelihood is strengthened by a Hoghton will which left an annuity to William Shakeshafte. There is also evidence that he went from Hoghton to join the players employed by Sir Thomas Hesketh at Rufford Hall. From there he is thought to have acquired an interest in the Globe Theatre.

HURST GREEN, NEAR WHALLEY
THE SHIREBURN ARMS

M6/M61 to J31, A59 to Whalley, B6246 to Gt Mitton. Turn left, B6243, and cross bridge. From Preston, B6243 via Elston and Grimsargh. From Burnley/Padiham, A671 into Whalley, then B6246.

With a pub name like this, one would expect to see coats of arms round every corner of the village, but there are only two examples of the Shireburn Arms here: one by bedroom 4 in the pub and the other at Stonyhurst College close by. In spite of this, the Shireburn name is very much part of the landscape, the history of Hurst Green and, of course, of the pub. The Shireburn Arms began life in 1697 when it was a farm with outbuildings. In those days, apart from farming, the main occupation was handloom weaving; later on mills were established around the village, driven by water power.

The great home of the Shireburns was begun in 1523, altered and extended by successive generations. Hurst Green was an estate village with almshouses built at Kemple End to care for the poor and sick; these were dismantled in the 1940s and re-erected at Hurst Green to serve as cottages for employees at Stonyhurst College, which was originally the Shireburn family home, sadly lost to them in the eighteenth century. At that time Sir Nicholas Shireburn's son and heir died through eating yew berries; on the death of Sir Nicholas his daughter inherited the house and estate, which passed on her death to the Weld family.

By 1831, then owned by the Welds, the pub buildings were sold and run as a hotel; the three buildings today give it a substantial appearance. Its role as a hotel in the nineteenth century was short, as the then proprietor's daughter inherited it; she

Three separate buildings combine to form the Shireburn Arms, well placed to visit Stonyhurst College.

A magnificent view of Stonyhurst.

was a Dominican nun and it became a convent in 1856. Ten years later it was sold to Stonyhurst College (of which more later), which in turn sold it in 1975.

It has been run as a hotel since then, with its facilities having been continuously improved. There are now eighteen comfortable bedrooms as well as the bar and lounges; the extensive Valley Restaurant with splendid views of the Ribble valley and the Pennines is much used for special events, the Shireburn Arms being licensed for civil wedding ceremonies.

Visitors to the Shireburn Arms can expect to find some activity going on around the pub at any time. Day courses include 'History around us, 2005', 'Countryside at the Shireburn, 2005' and 'Sketching and Painting'. The Shireburn is home to the famous Tolkien Trail; J.R.R. Tolkien, author of *Lord of the Rings*, used Hurst Green, the Shireburn and Stonyhurst College as inspiration for his most famous book.

A short walk from the pub to see the Shireburn Almshouses is well worthwhile and visitors should not miss a view of what is now Stonyhurst College and what was once the great home of the Shireburns offered to the Jesuits of Liège by Thomas Weld in 1794. It became the famous Roman Catholic school, and a number of the buildings were erected by the Jesuits, notably the Church of St Peter, which stands to the right of the gatehouse as seen from the avenue. It has a remarkable similarity to King's College Chapel in Cambridge.

There are many treasures in the fine library at the College, whose famous former pupils include Charles Laughton the actor and Sir Arthur Conan Doyle, author of the Sherlock Holmes stories, who based *The Hound of the Baskervilles* on Stonyhurst. Gerard Manley Hopkins, the poet, was a young priest here.

The Shireburn coat of arms.

The College is open to the public from time to time during the holidays: details can be obtained from tourist information centres and, of course, the Shireburn Arms.

This is not all, by any means. Whalley is not far away and the drive there crosses the river Hodder close to the point where it joins the Ribble. A spectacular packhorse bridge here over the Ribble familiarly known as 'Cromwell's Bridge', was built by Richard Shireburn in 1562. The name arises from the belief (probably unfounded) that Cromwell and his army crossed it on their way to Stonyhurst in 1648, where Cromwell stayed overnight before going on to defeat the King's army at Preston.

At Whalley are the ruins of Whalley Abbey (1296) and the even older parish church. In the church are choir stalls with beautiful misericords; these were originally made for the Abbey and were moved to the church after the Dissolution of the Monasteries. In the churchyard are three handsome tenth-century Celtic crosses.

If you have time left, go to see the Church of All Hallows at Great Mitton, where you will find the Shireburn Chapel and impressive monuments to the great family of Stonyhurst, whose house was lost but whose name is still very much alive.

LANCASTER: *THE SUN HOTEL & BAR*

M6 to J34, then A683 into A6 south. Follow one-way system to right turn (A6 north). Then King Street, China Street downhill. Safe parking on left opposite Church Street; or A6 north into King Street as above.

Although the original Sun Inn's history goes back a very long way, the present Sun Hotel & Bar is unlike any other pub in this book in that it is still taking on a new life and identity. The builders remain working, invisibly it is true, although the bar and restaurant have been fully operational for some time and in September 2005 eight totally redesigned and refurnished bedrooms were available. Twenty-four, including one with a four-poster bed, will be finished by the time this book is published.

The work being done is an archaeologist's dream, as one discovery after another confirms that, as at Bath, the remains of Roman buildings here were covered up by later developments. A Roman well was found and broken pottery of all kinds has been collected by the builders.

There is an impression of substantial stone walls everywhere, but at some time in the past the traditional 'wattle-and-daub' construction was used. An example is

The Sun Hotel today.

Left: Private dining room, once the servants' quarters. *Above:* Example of wattle-and-daub construction on one of the landings.

exposed on one of the landings and clearly the building was once timber framed. Much rebuilding must have taken place. Many stone fireplaces have been uncovered, ancient windows unblocked and doors revealed.

The inn was built on the site of Stoop Hall, a grand medieval hall shown on a Lancaster map of 1610 as New Hall. The Stoop Hall licence was recorded as early as 1680, the premises being renamed 'Sun Inn on Stoop Hall' in 1721. At that time the Sun stables occupied the rear of the buildings and the inn probably took its new name from the stables. It was not long before it became known by the shortened name Sun Inn; today it is the Sun Hotel & Bar, offering all the services expected under that name.

Before the Judges' Lodging was bought nearby, sheriffs entertained visiting dignitaries at the Sun Inn, the Port Commissioners used the Sun for their meetings until they moved to Glasson Dock, and the Lancaster Agricultural Society met there.

In November 1745 Generals of the Jacobean army were quartered at the Sun during the march south – and on their way back as they retreated from Derby. It was a place for social gatherings too, including the Musical Society and the Freemasons. Turner, the great painter, stayed at the Sun in 1812 when he was doing his sketches of Heysham.

During the time that there were stables in Sun Street, coaches would pull into the inn's courtyard and passengers were able to take refreshment in what is now the bar and restaurant. A side door near the bar provided access for coach passengers.

Today the main entrance is on Church Street; the whole area in front of, and around the bar is an open space furnished with tables and chairs and extending into the neighbouring premises. To the rear of this is more dining space and beyond is an attractive outdoor garden area. The servants' quarters of earlier days have been converted into a private dining room where an old well, carefully restored, can be viewed through a glass cover in the floor.

The quality and variety of works of modern art that have been selected to be shown at the Sun Hotel are worthy of a gallery collection and are an excellent solution to the problem of the form of decoration that extensive stone walls require.

Had the rebuilding of the Sun and the creating of its new image not been such a serious commercial enterprise it would have been tempting to call it a dream taking shape. It has demanded so much imagination to launch a new business for a particular market that it is far more; it represents a well-thought-out business plan, a determination to overcome difficulties – of which there have been plenty – and a confidence in the future. The number of customers, particularly in the evening, shows that this confidence is well placed; the comfortable bedrooms and the overnight bookings to date confirm the attraction of the Sun to Lancaster visitors.

The Sun Hotel is located close to some of the best tourist attractions in the city; the A6 through-route passes the corner of Church Street and 'Safe Parking' facilities are but a few steps away. The seventeenth-century Judges' Lodging Museum and Lancaster Castle are near neighbours, also Lancaster Priory Church, which has striking canopied choir stalls.

East of the city centre and well signed is Williamson Park, with the spectacular Ashton Memorial visible even from the motorway, and the Butterfly House. The views from here are remarkable.

The bar at the Sun.

LANCASTER, ALDCLIFFE ROAD: *THE WATER WITCH*

Good train services from Leeds and Preston. Waterbus daily service. M6 to J34, then A683 into A6 south. Parking by Penny Street Bridge.

Of the many canalside pubs in Lancashire, this is the most spectacular and now one of the most successful, though its history shows that this was not always the case. Naturally, without the Lancaster Canal there would never have been a pub here, so the story of the Water Witch has to begin after the canal's construction in the late eighteenth century.

The industrial demand for transport between Manchester, Preston, Lancaster and Kendal led to proposals for the building of a canal; John Rennie's survey was the basis for it, and construction began in 1792. Within seven years the canal between Preston and Tewitfield, south of Kendal, was opened, including a large aqueduct over the river Lune near Lancaster. The northern extension to Kendal was completed in 1819 and the branch to Glasson Dock was opened in 1826, with access to the sea. Sadly, the Tewitfield to Kendal section was closed in 1968 with the building of the M6.

The name Water Witch for the pub was not dreamed up by some modern PR consultant, as many people believe, but originated with Water Witch Waterbuses. And what an appropriate name it turned out to be! The waterbuses provided a daily service on the canal between Kendal and Preston in the early nineteenth century, doing the journey in fourteen hours, a time that was almost halved in 1833 to

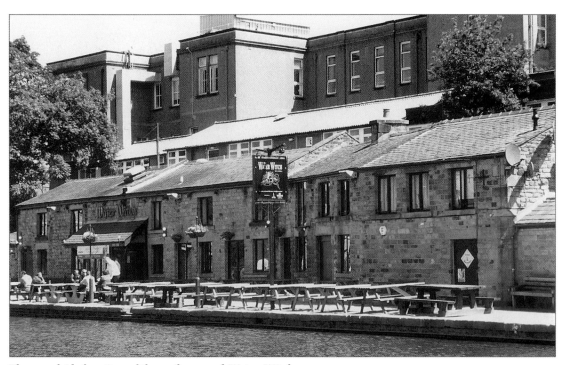

The canalside location of the aptly named Water Witch.

Moorings seen from the canal footbridge close to the Water Witch.

compete with the stagecoaches. A swift change of horses at Lancaster helped to achieve this, and 14,000 passengers were carried in the first six months of operation. The stables built at Lancaster for the service were eventually to become today's Water Witch pub.

It was the Westmorland Brewery that first took a Waterways lease on the property; the south end of the building was used for storage, and much of the rest remained a shell for some time. They were the first, in 1978, to use the name Water Witch for the pub they operated. On the collapse of the brewery the lease was sold to Yates's Wine Lodge, which introduced the restaurant and extended the cellars; in 1990 it was sold again, but competition and apparently a succession of poor managers resulted in its being put up for sale.

For two years the Water Witch appeared to have no future, then the directors of C2 Investment, a new company, who had met at Lancaster University and drank at the pub, set out to turn it around, having recalled what it had been and what it could be again. They acquired the site in February 2002.

The Water Witch is Lancaster's first true canalside pub; its long frontage stretches along the towpath with tables outside by the water and a conspicuous sign; a footbridge leads across the canal. There are moorings of all kinds and good photographic views in all directions.

Passengers ashore on Rennie's canal viaduct over the river Lune near Lancaster.

The Water Witch is built of stone, with flagstone floors, exposed rafters, pine panels and wall mirrors; the decor is modern and stylish, particularly featuring the stairway to a mezzanine floor mainly reserved for dining. Open all day, the pub is popular with students who appreciate the wide choice of beer and wines as well as the cheese and meat boards. There is a policy of traditional values and finest products; do not expect to find heavily advertised brands at the Water Witch.

Local reaction to the policies and products of the Water Witch has been very positive, awards numerous and continuing:

UK Wine Pub of the Year, 2003 (*Morning Advertiser* industry awards)
Perfect Pub of the Year, 2003, 2004 and 2005 (*Daily Telegraph* Granada Region
  sponsored by Abbott Ale)
Real Ale Pub of the Year, 2003 and 2004 (Lunesdale CAMRA branch)
Town Pub of the Year, 2004 (Lunesdale CAMRA Branch)
Best Pub award, Lancashire 2005–6 (*AA Good Pub Guide*)

There is convenient car parking behind the Lancaster Royal Infirmary, also bus stops there, only a short walk away. Of great importance to the Water Witch is the waterbus terminus, right outside the pub, bringing passengers from Carnforth, Bolton le Sands and Hest Bank. With a two-hour break here at Lancaster, returning passengers have time to take refreshment at the pub and do shopping as well.

A fascinating cruise is available from the Water Witch to the historic Lune Aqueduct, John Rennie's masterpiece of civil engineering. The journey, which includes a live commentary, also offers an opportunity to go ashore on the viaduct. The views of the city skyline and the river Lune below are breathtaking. What is more, the timing is perfect: lunch at the Water Witch, depart 13.00 on *Millennium Swiftsure* or *Swallow*, return to Water Witch 14.15. Still in time for more Lancaster!

There is, of course, a wide variety of visits in Lancaster itself: the seventeenth-century Judges' Lodging Museum and Lancaster Castle are near neighbours, as is Lancaster Priory Church.

LATHOM: *THE SHIP INN*

From Preston and Liverpool, A59 to Burscough Bridge. Between the two bridges and almost opposite the post office take School Lane. Continue, cross canal bridge, turn sharp right on to Wheat Lane (recommended route).

Close to Ring o'Bells Lane on the A5209 approaching Burscough is narrow Wheat Lane which immediately crosses an even narrower canal bridge. Within yards is a junction, not of a road or of a railway line, but where the Leeds and Liverpool Canal is joined by the Rufford Branch that goes on to Tarleton.

A delightful spot, now a conservation area, it has stone cottages, bridges and a series of locks; by the second lock is the Ship Inn at Lathom, called by CAMRA 'the gem of the area'. And so it is, white walled with welcoming seats outside and in the

The welcoming exterior of the Ship Inn at Lathom.

CROMWELL'S STONE
THIS STONE WAS RE-SITED HERE IN 1974
FROM TAMSTEADS, PART OF LATHOM WOOD
BY KIND PERMISSION OF THE FAMILY OF
THE LATE A. M. HUGHES, ESQ.
THE HOLLOWS IN THE STONE ARE SAID
TO HAVE BEEN USED FOR CASTING SHOT
USED BY CROMWELL'S ARMY IN THE SIEGE
OF LATHOM HOUSE 1644-45

garden. Nowadays the Ship's reputation is the enviable one of knowing its customers well. It is not common to find pubs in the food business which have so many and such regular 'regulars' that their tables are reserved as a matter of course unless a message comes in to say that someone cannot manage it today. There are the walkers, the fishermen, the golf ladies and, of course, the boat people, with the canal right behind the pub.

The boat people are the narrowboat weekenders or holidaymakers, not the nineteenth-century working bargees, whose thirst was legendary. They are long since gone, but brought the Ship's main business when the canal was used as a commercial waterway serving the needs of industry. Competition for moorings and for passage through the locks was fierce and apparently the cause of argument, sometimes violence, especially when drink had been flowing freely. Sometimes blood flowed freely, too, giving rise, or so it is said, to the Ship's local and familiar name 'The Blood Tub'.

Lathom Lock, Rufford branch, close to the Ship Inn.

Lathom's almshouses and little chapel.

More likely is the alternative explanation of the gory name which relies on the cottage at the end of the Ship building once occupied by a former landlady of the pub. She made quantities of black puddings and was always ready to do a deal, exchanging ale for buckets of pigs' blood, a vital ingredient. Whichever you believe, a nice story. Her cottage has now been incorporated into the pub itself as a restaurant. The domestic stove has been left where it had always been. Was that where the black puddings were cooked?

The cottage and the adjoining dining room lead to the bar, beyond which a passage lined with naval badges and canal paintings opens to a very cosy snug, then to the extension, the games room.

Such is the quality of food here (the fish is outstanding) as well as the ale that the Southport and District Branch of CAMRA voted the Ship Pub of the Year in 2004. A three-shift day has developed: lunchtime, naturally, then two hours or so at about five o'clock, followed by the younger clientele after 8 p.m. Fortunately the staff are happy to fit in with these peaks of business and the large car park facing the pub makes a visit a relaxing affair. Some people enjoy a walk along the canal towpath from Burscough; there is always activity on the water because of the lock gates immediately behind the Ship.

A pub that does not have a ghost. Now that's a change! At least, not one they can identify at the Ship, although the girls wonder what makes things fall off shelves without the help of human hands.

There is more to Lathom than the few cottages and the Ship along the canal; the ancient village and Lathom Park lie on the B5240, which runs south from the A5209 close to Ring o'Bells Lane. The only evidence of the once great Lathom House, home of the Stanleys, is a beautiful chapel and almshouses. Within the chapel are a lectern and screen brought from Burscough Priory after the Dissolution of the Monasteries.

The first Lathom House was destroyed by Cromwell's soldiers in 1645 after a siege; it was only six years later that James Stanley, Earl of Derby, was executed at Bolton outside the Old Man & the Scythe (see pp. 30–3). The house was rebuilt in 1720, but that, too, has gone. The estate was eventually sold in 1924.

No visitor to the Ship should miss an opportunity to go to Martin Mere, the Wildfowl and Wetlands Centre, which is only about 2 miles away, taking a turning off the A59 at Burscough Bridge. Just follow the brown signs.

This huge reserve, covering 370 acres, is one of Britain's most important wetland sites. The pathways are planned so that you can go on a 'journey round the world' and observe exotic birds all the way. In winter the reserve welcomes thousands of pink-footed geese, whooper and Bewick's swans, among many other species. You can feed some of the birds by hand.

There is convenient access for visitors with disabilities, including a free wheelchair loan arrangement. Needless to say there is every facility for visitors at Martin Mere: toilets, a children's play area and a cafeteria with a wide menu. Guide dogs are allowed in the grounds.

LIMBRICK NEAR RIVINGTON: *THE BLACK HORSE*

From north, M61 to J8. Take A6 through Chorley, fork left A673.
At Anderton crossroads turn left. Keep left on Long Lane with M61 below.
Pub on right in Limbrick, car park opposite.
From south, M61 to J6, turn left on A6027. At roundabout turn right, A6 to
Adlington. At Railway Street turn right, cross A673 at Anderton. Follow Long
Lane as above.

It is a sad fact that we are steadily losing pubs, both in town and country, as they close their doors for the last time. Even whole villages have been under threat for a variety of reasons, perhaps because they stand in the way of a water project and some, indeed, have ended up at the bottom of a reservoir.

Limbrick's address 'near Rivington' is a reminder of the vast reservoirs in the area and while not fearing the worst, there seems to be a need for reassurance that the pub is safe and flourishing, which it is!

There are only about 100 yards of the village on Long Lane as it slopes down to the narrow stone bridge over the river Yarrow. Happily it has survived, although the landlord reckons that there are now only about a dozen houses: of those, most are

Rivington reservoir and, below, the Black Horse.

The neat little bar at the Black Horse.

restorations and rebuilds with extensions. The village did very nearly die – and the Black Horse with it – when factories in towns using water, then steam power, put the handloom weavers and part-time farmers out of business and, one suspects, the blacksmith and shopkeeper too.

People left Limbrick to seek work elsewhere, to the point where the population had declined to a handful – fewer than forty. There is no doubt that the Black Horse was a farmstead as well as an inn; it stands right on the roadside with land behind it and river water only yards away.

Today it is an unassuming, plain, stone-built pub; its interior is equally modest, with a small bar, three rooms on the front, including a games room, and one at the back. The walls are massively thick and the windows are small; the low, beamed ceilings and mainly settle furniture create a homely atmosphere.

Visitors have been welcomed here for a very long time; the pub is believed to have been licensed originally by the Leyland magistrates in 1577, which could make the Black Horse one of the first recorded pubs in Lancashire. If Thomas Burke, researcher and author, is correct, an inn stood here before 1066: a very long history. There has, of course, been much rebuilding of the pub since 1577.

What is particularly interesting is that visitors to the Black Horse are welcomed by each other as well as by the landlord. Perhaps it was my lucky day, but everyone seemed intrigued that they were in a truly historic place – so much so that it was to be featured in a book and they might just star in a photograph. Few came from close by, but had come out for a ride or for a walk on the moors, and not for the first time – that was obvious. A lot of people come regularly because the Black Horse is set in dramatic countryside and has that vital combination of a warm welcome and fine food. The meat-and-potato pie and peas is magic. All this and history too!

No doubt Thomas Burke had noticed the unusual village name of Limbrick along with others in Lancashire like Norbreck and Scarisbrick. All will have been tenth-century Norse settlements, the Scandinavian 'brekka' meaning 'slope'. 'Lim' could be a family name or some feature that identified the place. In such an isolated place intermarriage must have been common; certainly until the depopulation of the nineteenth century a common family name was Catterall. Since then things have changed with the coming of the railways, and now the M61. Round the corner of Long Lane, Back Lane is unbelievably bridged by the concrete supports of the motorway.

The crossroads below the Black Horse is signed Chorley to the left and Anglezarke to the right – another Norse name, given to the reservoir and the moors beyond. The winding lane towards Anglezarke eventually crosses the reservoir to a picnic area; uphill the road leads to the moors. The views from the moors are magnificent, as are the walks on the shoreline of the reservoir.

LYDIATE: *THE SCOTCH PIPER INN*

M6 to J26, M58 to end, A59 to Maghull, fork left, A5147.
From Liverpool, A59 north to Maghull, fork left, A5147.
From Preston, A59 south; at roundabout near Aughton, B5407. Then at
Lydiate, A5147 north (Southport road).

If you walk north along the Southport road in Lydiate, the Scotch Piper is close to Lolly's bridge over the Leeds and Liverpool canal. Bus stop signs on the road say 'Merseytravel', so where are we? 'In Lancashire, of course,' said the landlord. 'Old Lancashire, that is, before they played about with the boundary.' As it happens, the 'new' Lancashire county boundary is only a matter of yards up the road beyond the Scotch Piper.

The sign by the pub door says 'The oldest inn in Lancashire AD1320', so perhaps the landlord feels the need to clarify things before a visitor lodges a protest. What a pub this is! Everyone said do not miss the Scotch Piper. It is in the *Good Beer Guide* and is listed in the CAMRA National Inventory. Sound advice, then.

Standing back from the road, white walled, with a thatched roof (now with a proud new ridge), it is a small traditional domestic building unaltered, it would seem, since it was built – that is, until you walk nearer and see the massive buttresses that were needed recently to support the pub's front wall which was showing dangerous signs of weakness. Structural problems are to be expected in such an ancient building; 1320 may refer to its predecessor and there may have been a rebuild, but very old it certainly is.

The pleasing exterior of the Scotch Piper.

The gables were built on the cruck system that medieval builders used. They chose timbers that curved left and right to form arches rising from ground level to create gables and support the roof timbers – crude, but effective. The right-end crucks have gone with an extension to the building; other alterations and restorations after fires have taken place, but it remains a unique example of an early medieval yeoman's dwelling. Without doubt it was both an ale-house and a small farm in its early days in order to provide a living.

There are several legends associated with the Scotch Piper – one that it was constructed round an oak tree which served as a support for the building. Its former name, the Royal Oak, is often quoted as confirmation of this, but it is the unusual crucks that seem to have misled the creators of the legend.

The fine Scotch Piper pub sign is a link with another legend that retreating Scottish soldiers came this way after Bonnie Prince Charlie's army abandoned its march on London in 1745. Having reached Derby, the Scottish troops lost the will to continue, so it is quite plausible that stragglers passed through Lydiate on their way home.

One of these may have stopped at the pub for rest and refreshment – indeed may have stayed and may have married the landlord's daughter – a very nice story! If the pub then became the Bagpiper or Highland Piper, we have a really happy ending, even if the name eventually had a further change.

The entrance door is now at the left-hand end of the building, with the tiny servery, hardly a bar, immediately inside. All three rooms lead off to the right, the furthest furnished and carpeted in mainly modern style, while the first two 'bays' of the house really show its age, with dark beams, flagged floors and basic furniture.

The Scotch Piper's central room with its massive, dark timbers.

Two is a crowd in the Scotch Piper's bar: it's no more than a servery really.

The remains of St Catherine's Chapel.

The central room has extraordinary timbers, some of which may have been introduced to enhance its atmosphere, but as a fragment of history the Scotch Piper is impressive.

The tenancies of the Moorcroft family have been record-breaking. Generation after generation took over the pub until the end of the Second World War; in 1961, after several changes, Charles and Ada Rigby took over and on Charles's death in 1996 his brother Fred Rigby and his wife Anne-Marie became the licensees, and still are. A family business yet again!

When you visit, look for the lovely painting in the extension room of a ruined church with the Scotch Piper in the background. The painter has used his skill and some imagination by including the pub, which is not precisely where he portrays it. Never mind, because the subject is next door, behind high hedges and trees but miraculously open to the public, an experience not to be missed if you are willing to walk just a few yards up the road.

St Catherine's Chapel was built for the private worship of the Ireland family, who were lords of the manor at Lydiate for four centuries. The chapel dates from the late fifteenth century and was damaged at the Reformation. There is evidence that secret Catholic worship took place there for many years. What a beautiful ruin!

Each year there is a Shakespeare play in the chapel precincts and a more appropriate place for it would be difficult to imagine. Details and tickets can be obtained from the Scotch Piper.

LYTHAM, HENRY STREET
THE TAPS INN

M6 to J32, then M55, or A6 to M55 at J1. M55 to J4, then continue on B5230. Turn left on to B5261 (Blackpool Road). Continue into Church Road, Lytham.

A few yards away from busy Clifton Square and one block (as the Americans say) from Lytham Green and the river Ribble, the Taps Inn cannot claim to have a particularly favourable position. Its front does not have outstanding design features and double yellow lines discourage car parking anywhere near. Yet it is one of the most successful and interesting pubs in Lytham.

Ask most people what they remember of Lytham and they will reply without hesitation the Windmill and the Old Lifeboat Station on Lytham Green. Yet in the district there is a belief that soup at the Taps is even more popular and familiar than the Windmill. 'Everyone goes for the soup', they said, so I did. I was foolish enough to ask if there was a choice. 'Yes', said the man at the bar. 'Soup, or soup and a roll.' It was meat and vegetable that day; both soup and roll were memorable – home-made, everyone assured me.

The Taps was once a row of cottages built to house the ostlers employed at the 1800 Clifton Arms Hotel in coaching days. The men were conveniently located across the courtyard at the rear of the hotel and would have been readily on call. Some one hundred years ago, ostlers having had their day, a new use was found for the premises: they became a bar or tap for the hotel, hence the name. In those days

Unassuming yet popular, in spite of the double yellow lines. The soup is a great attraction.

men still touched their caps and children curtseyed when their 'betters' passed by, so it was entirely proper for labourers and artisans to have a separate place to drink. They could have it at the bar, or take it home in a jug from the out-sales counter; at that time the separate rooms in the cottages had been retained. Today the pub is almost one big room, although small bays are popular for groups such as Probus after their meetings. Rotary and Masonic meals take place at the Clifton Arms, after which members cross to the Taps for their drinks.

Although there are padded seats and chairs, tables are basic with plain softwood tops, the walls are lined with row after row of beer bottles of all kinds and labels. The landlord wants to offer real ale and has his own brew, 'Taps Best', brewed specially at Stoke-on-Trent.

The special deal the landlord has struck allows him to go as far away as Bury St Edmunds for Greene King, or to Keighley for Timothy Taylor favourites. He is a quality man and his cellar confirms it: immaculate, well organised and so cool.

Although lunchtime customers, including family groups, are mainly of retirement age, there is plenty for sports enthusiasts, including TV facilities. A good collection of team photographs is on display; hockey is obviously a popular sport and a number of clubs hold their meetings at the Taps. Sports celebrities use the pub as their local; Bill Beaumont, once an England Rugby international, is a regular here.

A few yards away from the Taps at the corner of Henry Street is the Lytham Heritage Centre. Available there are books and leaflets about Lytham; one, published by the Lytham Heritage Group, is entitled *A Walk around Lytham's Heritage*, and is invaluable to the visitor. The cover carries a fine line-drawing of the windmill, has an excellent map and a commentary for the walk.

The Taps is noted for its huge collection of beer bottles lining the walls.

A lasting memory for visitors: the windmill on Lytham Green.

One of the most surprising historic memorials at Lytham is on the roadside near St Cuthbert's Parish Church, where St Cuthbert's Cross on Church Road marks the spot where the body of St Cuthbert is said to have rested on its way for burial at Durham Cathedral.

Beginning at Clifton Square, with its modern pebble mosaic, there are interesting landmarks on the walk from all stages of Lytham's history. The town's fishing heritage is illustrated, and its growth into a holiday resort. By the nineteenth century hotels such as the Clifton Arms were receiving visitors by stagecoach from several Lancashire towns; at that time bathing was becoming very popular, and the ostlers at the Taps were fully occupied. Later the railways brought many more holidaymakers from farther afield; St Annes developed alongside its older neighbour Lytham and became a place to stay – and to which to retire.

MIDDLETON, GREATER MANCHESTER
YE OLDE BOAR'S HEAD

From Manchester, A665 Cheetham Hill Road to Broughton Park/Crumpsall.
Turn right, A576 Middleton Road to M60, J19.
From M62, J18, take M60 to J19.
From Bury, M66 to M60, J19.
Then all routes A576; at Middleton Shopping Centre turn right. Follow Oldham Road A576 to 2nd roundabout. Turn left into Assheton Way, car park at Market Place. Long Street opposite, pub 100 yards opposite library.

Everyone knows what happens when some local feature, even an old, well-loved part of the landscape, stands in the way of a scheme dreamed up by a powerful group of councillors: 'It will have to go!' This was very nearly the fate of the Boar's

The magnificent exterior of Ye Olde Boar's Head.

Head, one of the few surviving old buildings in the town, in the early twentieth century, when Middleton Town Council proposed to erect a new town hall. A fate worse than this for such a purpose could hardly be imagined. Fortunately good sense prevailed; the Boar's Head not only survived but was so well refurbished that it received an award in the *1991 Good Pub Guide* for the Best Pub Restoration of the Year.

The half-timbered building goes back to the middle of the sixteenth century. A date on a stone lintel in the cellar corresponds to this; other evidence confirms that part of the pub was on the site in 1600 and possibly earlier. It once consisted of two buildings, probably dwelling houses.

It stands on a sloping site, and the stone base of the walls must have replaced the original some long time ago, perhaps when the supports at the building's corners were added. The buttresses at the corner of Long Street and Durnford Street are very noticeable, and the room on the corner is the oldest part of the pub. The corner room has some very ancient timbers in it, as old as the twelfth century, clearly reused from some demolished building.

From the time of Cromwell Ye Olde Boar's Head was used as a sessions court and when petty sessions were located at Middleton in the nineteenth century they were held in a large room at the upper end of the site now known as the Sessions Room. This is used today for receptions and functions. Its huge fireplace has boars' heads cut into the stone, together with the date 1587; it would appear to have been brought to the Sessions Room from elsewhere. Smaller, but also very old, is the upstairs fireplace in a room used for 'events' and entertainment.

The outstanding interior features of the pub are the black iron fireplaces and the wealth of timbering. The stairs at the Durnford Street corner have a most beautiful carved newel post; the timbered arches at doorways and those dividing the interior have been preserved to give a strong feel of history. At the same time all the facilities and furnishings of a comfortable, modern pub have been added tastefully.

Unusually, there is a lunchtime carvery between the Durnford Street end of the building and the bar. Very popular orders for families are from the range of hot meat sandwiches and salads. The Boar's Head would always have been important for travellers needing food, especially when turnpike trusts improved roads and regular coach services began. In the nineteenth century the Manchester to Rochdale coach stopped at the pub in both directions; it had the impressive title of Middleton's first post house, with stabling for horses.

The Boar's Head is a place to explore, as there are so many small rooms. One of these is called the Sam Bamford Room (from the conversation there it could well be called the 'philosophy room'). Sam was born in Middleton in 1788 and was educated at Manchester Grammar School; apprenticed as a handloom weaver, he began to write and went to London to sell his poems. Loathing the restrictions that bound people to their workplace, he became a wanderer and an enthusiastic radical; his forthright views in support of social reform resulted in prison sentences, but today his portrait hangs beside those of Earl Grey, William Ewart Gladstone and the Duke of Devonshire in Manchester Reform Club.

The fireplace in the Sessions Room.

The Durnford Street corner with timbered arch and stairs. The newel post is exquisitely carved.

A room named for Sam Bamford. Born in 1788 he was a local poet and social reformer. Copies of his poems are on the walls.

Poetry reading takes place in the Sam Bamford Room every month; on the walls are copies of his poems such as 'Tim Bobbin's Grave'. Two verses of this in dialect read as follows:

> I stood beside Tim Bobbin's grave,
> 'At looks o'er Ratchda' teawn
> An' th'owd lad woke within his yerth
> An' sed wheer arto' beawn.
> I brought him op o'a deep breawn jug,
> 'At a gallon did contain,
> An' he took it at one blessed draught
> An' laid him deawn again.

One of the regulars in the Sam Bamford Room confessed that he loved Sam's work, but didn't always understand it!

Another room with an appealing atmosphere is that used by the Middleton Angling Society, with displays of fishing gear of all kinds and photographs of members past and present.

It is the past, present and future that come together so comfortably at the Boar's Head, both in the pub itself and in the family groups having time out together. Manchester, with all its attractions, is so close that it can easily be taken for granted – and rarely visited unless to entertain a guest.

ORMSKIRK
THE BUCK I'TH' VINE (formerly THE ROEBUCK)

From Preston and Liverpool, A59T; or M6 to J27, then A5209/59T.
Parking: From Preston and north, A59T into Burscough Road/Street. At
library turn left, then right into Wheatsheaf Car Park.
From Liverpool, A59T, fork right into Aughton Street. Turn left on A570T
(Southport Road). Car parks near parish church (The Stiles).

They say at the Buck that there was a pub on the site in 1641; others give a date of 1650, but so far back, nine years here or there make little difference. Rooms at the back of the pub were added much later and now provide games and TV, as well as a large lounge.

Entering from Burscough Street, without doubt the most historic street in the town and once the main Preston to Liverpool highway through Ormskirk, one finds the bar on the right of the corridor. For a moment you feel that it might be a converted Edwardian sweetshop with its curved window under which you place your drinks order. Behind the bar counter is a small parlour where once the privileged friends of the landlord would have been invited to sit.

The forecourt of the Buck I'th' Vine facing Burscough Street.

Ordering drinks at the Buck I'th' Vine's little bar is just like going to the counter in an old-fashioned sweetshop.

Moving across the corridor from the bar to the smoke room, you are really entering a separate building, as the pub's corridor is a converted former outside passageway. There were a number of these in Ormskirk, especially between the shops on Burscough Street, some surviving, such as Mystic Mews, facing the pub. There is currently a pet shop at the corner; at one time there were small shops of all kinds along these 'ginnels', but few remain today. The passageway at the Buck I'th' Vine is now roofed over and incorporated into the pub building that has taken over for its smoke room part of what was a shop next door.

Coaches would have used this passage to reach the rear courtyard where passengers alighted and boarded.

Stop right here! The glass panel of the smoke-room door will probably be covered with an advertising poster of some kind. Why that should be is one of life's mysteries, because it is one of the best examples of etched glass mentioned in this book.

It has, of course, the name 'Smoke Room'; this is combined in deep relief with the Buck I'th' Vine sign. Ask to see and feel this piece of work; perhaps if enough visitors do so the landlord will be able to achieve his ambition to cover the back with a white surface and to illuminate it. It deserves that.

The bar, the parlour and the smoke room door may have been a surprise, but we are not outside yet. The L-shaped pub building provides a spacious cobbled forecourt; the absence of motor traffic on Burscough Street is encouraging more and more people to eat and drink outside, as they can also at the rear.

The Buck I'th' Vine has the classic coaching-inn layout with a wide side entrance for coaches to swing in, a large courtyard for horses to be stabled and space for all the activities entailed in changing the horses. Not least, passengers needed to be fed quickly to avoid delaying the coaches. Some passengers stayed overnight: travel was dangerous – even more perilous at night.

There were up to thirty coach departures from Ormskirk every day, leaving the various inns, including the Buck I'th' Vine, and taking passengers to Lancaster and Preston, even to London. In addition there were commercial services with their own departure timetables, taking business and domestic goods. Loading was done at the inns used by the carriers, including the Buck I'th' Vine.

Looking round the courtyard, it is easy to identify the stables and also the brewhouse. They brewed their own beer here long ago, having their own malthouse some 300 years old, next door. One large building, now in poor condition, is called a store house, probably for want of a better title; we know that at one time the pub had its own theatre. This building was certainly more than a store house in the past, as it has its own minstrels' gallery.

Ormskirk has its own street market founded in 1286 by the monks of Burscough Abbey. Its focus is round the Clock Tower at the bottom of Burscough Street and is held on Thursdays. Ormskirk has parking restrictions on Thursdays and Saturdays. On other days the one-way traffic system and the parking arrangements are more convenient.

OVERTON: *THE GLOBE*

M6/A6 to Lancaster, continue north through city centre. Take A683 Morecambe road to roundabout, continue left on A683. At Heysham roundabout turn left, Middleton road. On into Overton, to Globe and access road to Sunderland.

To the casual passer-by, the Globe with its large conservatory and white-painted fence could not possibly qualify as a historic pub. Yet it does, having been built in the 1600s and, standing at the 'gateway' to Sunderland Point, will have seen history being made.

Overton is more isolated than most villages because the road from the north is cut off from time to time by high tides; to the east and west the by-roads go nowhere and to the south the road past the Globe to Sunderland is under water twice every day

The Globe is the 'gateway' to Sunderland Point. Check on tide times before going further.

The shoreline at Sunderland.

when the tide comes in. So, like a visit to Lindisfarne in Northumberland, you need to plan your journey with care. The bar at the Globe is the right place to ask for advice, as they keep a copy of the tide tables there.

With six en-suite bedrooms as well as a spacious bar and the convervatory the Globe is well able to offer hospitality both to holidaymakers and regulars. The pub is open all day, every day, for food and drink and there is a large car park just across the road. On the edge of the parking area the river Lune Millennium Park has one of its information points, not only giving general information about the area, but also what wildlife can be seen.

Overton is just a small village with one main street; its eighteenth-century cottages are white painted and decorated with flowers in the summer. Many visitors pass through without seeing Chapel Lane leading to the twelfth-century St Helen's Church, well worth a visit. Employment has, over the centuries, been dependent on farming and fishing, particularly for Lune salmon, which is a local delicacy. Ask for it at the Globe; if it is in season it will make your day.

Sunderland, part of Overton parish, which you must see, became a busy port in the eighteenth century and ships were built for Lancaster merchants for trade with the West Indies. Although there were two inns at Sunderland (both now gone), the Globe would have seen many sailors home from the West Indies and America.

At the turn of the century the Overton Pleasure Gardens became a fashionable place to go. A picture of the Gardens is in the bar and would have brought good business to the Globe. Today's visitors are attracted by the scenery of the estuary, the bird life and the opportunity to go to Sunderland Point, with its fascinating history.

The road sign facing the Globe is not very encouraging! Its message is 'Beware: Fast Tides, Hidden Channels and Quick Sands'. Further warnings on the way to Sunderland tell motorists of dangerous sections of the road when incoming tide water makes it too risky to proceed. It is 1¼ miles in all. Given the right precautions it is an experience that should not be missed; parking high up on the foreshore by the Information Point is safe.

Sunderland (the separated land) has always existed courtesy of the tides; until about 1715 there may have been no community there at all, such were the difficulties. At that time a Quaker, Robert Lawson, began building a village at Sunderland. The family were merchants and, following a voyage from Lancaster to the West Indies and back in 1687 by a small trading ship, the practice grew of merchants sharing in the cost and risk of journeys across the Atlantic to return with cargoes of sugar. Within a few years cargoes were being unloaded at a jetty at Sunderland and taken on to Lancaster by lighters or horse and cart. This avoided taking ships up the difficult channel of the Lune to the city. Soon mahogany from Barbados was being shipped for the Gillow family of Lancaster, whose furniture business was to become world famous.

By 1715 facilities at Sunderland were growing apace: a warehouse and even a modest ship-building and repair business had been established, sufficient to support a new community. The sea was the basis of its prosperity; it became a thriving port and, later, a bathing resort. The Old Hall, built at Sunderland Point, was one of several large houses, and there were, of course, the two pubs, the Ship Inn and the Maxwell Arms.

The simple grave of the black cabin boy who died here in 1736.

Sadly, Sunderland's prosperity was not to last: port development at Lancaster and the building of Glasson Dock in 1787 saw to that. Even the village's brief life as a holiday resort came to an end with the growing popularity of Morecambe.

The scenery remains as beautiful as ever. Boat people still enjoy the water and Sunderland is a favourite with bird watchers: redshank, golden plover, lapwing and dunlin are to be seen, the best time being about three hours before or after high tide. Remember the tide times!

Many visitors staying at the Globe go to Sunderland because they have heard of Sambo. He was a sea captain's black servant or cabin boy who came from the West Indies with his master in 1736. He died soon afterwards; some believed that he starved himself, or, thinking that he had been abandoned when his master went away, died of a broken heart. It is perhaps more likely that he died of some fever against which he had no immunity.

It was not possible at that time for him to have a grave in consecrated ground, so he was buried in the shelter of a wall in a field on the west shore. Turn on to the marked bridleway at the corner of what was once the Ship Inn on the sea front and follow it to the end between high hedges; turn left on the shore and the grave is a few steps away. A memorial stone was placed on the plot some years after he died, but after all this time feelings still run deep about him. He has a simple cross surrounded by painted pebbles, and flowers are regularly placed there by children. You are likely to meet other visitors coming or going if you make the pilgrimage to this pathetic little corner.

PRESTON, 166 FRIARGATE: *THE BLACK HORSE*

From the railway station turn right along Fishergate. In about ½ mile turn left into Cheapside/Friargate.
By car from M6 J29 (also from Chorley/Bamber Bridge); or M6 to J32 (also M55 from Blackpool).
There is also a Park & Ride stop in Lancaster Road near the Harris Museum & Art Gallery just east of Cheapside.

Because of alterations carried out on thousands of pubs in recent years, the number whose interiors might be considered of outstanding heritage interest has dwindled to fewer than 250. That is the considered view of CAMRA. One of the group's declared concerns has always been to defend Britain's traditional pubs as well as its traditional beers; its National Inventory is a pioneering initiative for bringing greater recognition and protection to Britain's most priceless historic pubs.

Suffice to say that the Black Horse is in that Inventory and is a very worthy representative of Preston's pubs for inclusion in this book. Space in the Inventory only allows for a one-line entry, but what follows here allows justice to be done.

A more prominent site would be difficult to imagine: a corner position fronting both Orchard Street and Friargate, a busy pedestrianised thoroughfare. In fact, the pub has three doors, all on different streets, which must be a unique feature.

Externally, as Pevsner would say, it is 'unfortunate', in having had a misguided modernisation in 1898. Mercifully the early interior was retained to delight our eyes today. Going back over two hundred years the pub was known as the Black Horse and Rainbow, and was popular enough in 1796 for Sir Edward Stanley to encourage its regulars by financial inducements to support the Whigs in what was considered the most corrupt election ever held in England.

The curved bar counter fronted with moulded ceramic tiles is quite extraordinary, both for size and visual effect. Together with its art nouveau stained glass and

The exterior of the Black Horse.

The Black Horse's remarkable bar.

lighting, it almost defies description; in a wild moment one could almost imagine an organist seated at the mighty Wurlitzer rising like magic to the acclaim of a cinema audience. Stained glass is everywhere and, not to be outdone, the tilers decorated the walls as well, while there is an attractive mosaic tiled floor.

At the right-hand side of the bar are framed awards received by the Black Horse for its interior, including that from CAMRA, its English Heritage Pub Design Award 1996: High Commended.

On the pub counter flap is a poster advertising the Preston Royal Hippodrome Theatre and one of its shows, *See how they run* (second year at the Comedy Theatre, London). Since the Hippodrome closed in 1957, the show must date from the 1950s or even earlier. The Hippodrome with its pavement canopy stood next door to the Black Horse (Wilkinson's store is now on that site), so the pub was nicely placed for the audience to rush out at the interval or at the end of the show for a drink. How convenient the Black Horse's three doors must have been! Perhaps the sudden surge of business at times like that explains the notice close to the Hippodrome poster urging people to know what they want and not to change their minds. No doubt performers and musicians also came for refreshment, lending support to the suggestion that the Black Horse at that time had a rather 'luvvie' bar.

The wall displays are intriguing: photographs of the old days, of course, and a framed programme for Preston Races, 1830. A copy of a 1907 document lists the pubs

The exceptional stained glass at the Black Horse has mercifully survived.

and brewers, when there were 435+ hotels, inns, taverns and beer-houses in Preston. The population then was 117,000, giving one pub per 269 persons, a lower figure than anywhere except Southampton. Perhaps that tells us something about Preston.

A 'regular' sitting just inside the door murmured that 1907 must have been a good year for a pub crawl and that if you haven't tried Old Tom, you haven't lived. Old Tom, brewed by Robinson's Brewery of Stockport, was, according to a beer mat, entered into the head brewer's handwritten notebook in 1899, illustrated with the cat's face. Today its gravity is still high at 8.5, ample evidence of its description as a strong ale. So strong indeed that landlord Keith has continued the custom of serving halves only. He insists that this is a winter brew, beyond the ability of new, especially young, drinkers to handle it if served in pints.

Occasionally the local CAMRA branch holds a meeting at the Black Horse, one of the only two pub entries in the Lancashire section of the CAMRA National Inventory. It is a great asset to the city and should be visited, especially if Old Tom is in season.

RIBCHESTER: *THE WHITE BULL*

M6 to J31, A59. In about 5 miles turn left, B6245; or M65 to J6, A6119 to A666 at Wilpshire, then B6245.

Ribchester's very name, like that of Lancaster, spells out 'Roman'. Although there is evidence of earlier peoples here, it was geography and the Romans that put Ribchester firmly on the map. First to conquer, then to rule, the Romans needed roads and military posts; on the legions' military route north they met a barrier – the river

Ribble. If it could be forded that would be their preferred way onwards and the crossing would need to be defended, hence Ribchester and its fort, built in about AD 80.

Most of the Roman settlement has been lost through erosion by the river and from stone robbing. Later development of the village on top of Roman remains has concealed much of interest, too, but the White Bull gives a hint of what Roman Ribchester was like. Its porch is supported by four Tuscan columns from the fort, possibly from a temple; like a number of Roman buildings, the temple could have been washed away by the river in flood.

The front of the White Bull seems very familiar, as it has been photographed so often. The date 1707 is marked, but the pub is probably a good deal older and, once seen, is always remembered, with its mounting-block beside the porch. Above it the carved white bull is even more prominent than the usual hanging sign close to it.

Hardly noticeable when looking at the front of the pub are the two extensions: to the left the old stables with a tethering ring in the wall has become a games room, and a former shop to the right is now incorporated and is a handsome dining room. Intriguing in April 2005 was a big notice bearing the words 'The fox is back'. The mystery was solved by the landlord, who had two halves of a stuffed fox on his desk. For many years a curio at the White Bull, one half of the fox was on one side of the wall beside the main stairs, the other half on the opposite side, the fox apparently

A well-remembered porch to the pub, with its prominent carved white bull and the Roman pillars on both sides of the entrance.

'The fox is back.'

jumping through the wall. Recovered by the police as mysteriously as it was stolen three years or so ago, it was about to be restored to its place of honour and the notice was intended to inform the world – or at least Ribchester – that the fox had been recovered.

The extensions at both ends of the bar area give that feeling of separate rooms so sadly lost in many pubs. A rear staircase leads to the bedrooms and if you are interested in Roman Ribchester, the rear bedroom looks down on the pub garden with outdoor seating; over the wall is a good view of the uncovered Roman baths.

Like a number of country pubs, the White Bull once served as a courthouse; for that reason a room was used as a cell for prisoners. The cellars are, without doubt, very old, but not Roman. Only a stone's throw from the river bank, whatever building stood here in Roman times would have seen an army marching northwards up Water Street after crossing the river by the ford.

The Roman bathhouse at Ribchester.

The river Ribble and Pendle Hill.

Most of the important Roman buildings lay below or near the parish church, St Wilfrid's, which dates from 1193. It has a link with the de Hoghton family and the Royal Oak (pp. 86–9); look for their 'cage pew' separated from the south aisle by a beautifully carved fourteenth-century screen. Both the church and the neighbouring Ribchester Museum are within a few yards of the village school and the White Bull. A visit to church and museum is highly recommended.

A pathway and gate from the river frontage by the school lead down to the river inlet that provides a connection with the Roman baths behind the White Bull. The baths have been fully excavated, showing the baths of various temperatures and the furnace room. A medieval well close by has also been uncovered.

The White Bull stands just where Water Street and Church Street join, forming a small square which represents the centre of the village, although there has never been a market there. Like many Lancashire villages Ribchester had the usual variety of craftsmen and traders to meet local needs. Agricultural work was available and by the seventeenth century flax spinning and weaving took place in the cottages. By the eighteenth century flax had been replaced by cotton and linen was no longer produced at Ribchester.

Weavers' cottages near the White Bull survive today; as good light was needed for weaving in the so-called loomshops, they had large windows, sometimes several of them. Another important requirement was humidity to avoid damage to yarn in the weaving process; this was usually carried out at the rear of cottages where the old loomshops are now hidden from view.

Sometimes the loomshops were in cellars, an example of this is just off the Square near the White Bull; opposite are examples of second-floor windows of rooms that were probably used for preparing yarn for weaving down below.

Sadly, the factory system destroyed domestic spinning and weaving by the middle 1800s and there was great hardship in Ribchester. Although two mills opened in Ribchester, many people had to find work elsewhere. It has taken a long time for employment to recover, and nowadays tourism provides most of the work in the village. Such is Ribchester's attraction and its small size that a day visitor can see and appreciate most of its history and, of course, that of the White Bull.

If you are fortunate enough to be on the river frontage towards the end of the day, linger for a few moments to look upstream in a north-easterly direction. In the distance, changing light, shadows and colours on Pendle Hill will give you a magic moment.

ROCHDALE: *THE ROEBUCK*

Regular train services from Manchester Victoria.
Bus and tram services from Lancashire towns.
By car: M62 to J20, then A627M. At roundabout join A58 signed Town
Centre. At Town Centre lights turn right signed Town Hall. Good parking at
Town Hall.

Close to Rochdale's majestic Town Hall, the Roebuck is easily found. Either go through an archway next to the Yorkshire Bank on Yorkshire Street, or from Newgate via an unofficial parking area close to Yates's Wine Lodge.

Rochdale's Roebuck has so many close neighbours that it is impossible to take a photograph to do it justice.

The Telegraph Lounge at the Roebuck.

Now almost overwhelmed by newer and massive town-centre buildings so close that an outside photograph of the pub is hardly practicable, here is a fine example of a busy and popular pedestrian local. In such a congested location it is perhaps just as well that an extension to the premises is not needed.

Popular, certainly, with the Roebuck's clientele comfortably divided between the bar area for the regular pint of bitter drinkers in T-shirt, jeans and trainers and the lounge at the back for readers of the *Daily Telegraph* with their modest halves of lager and lime and ladies with shopping bags and their gin and tonics.

The decor is art nouveau throughout: stained-glass windows with long green and blue floral designs, matching carpeting and curtains. The mahogany bar has lamps of the same art nouveau style as the rest of the public area. One very obvious difference is in the wall decoration: in the bar plain emulsion over a figured wallpaper, while the lounge has a patterned wallpaper of the kind made popular by William Morris.

Much of what can be seen is the result of refurbishment in the last twenty years and a development of the food side of the pub's business to take advantage of its town-centre location and lunch breaks. Change is inevitable to meet changing needs and change has been a feature of the Roebuck's life for many years. In fact, it has had two sites and two names: for convenience, the 'Old' Roebuck and the 'New' Roebuck.

A framed copy of an auction sale notice dated 15 June 1780 is on the wall of today's Roebuck. It refers to the sale of a Roebuck Inn, almost certainly the original, or 'Old' Roebuck, then occupied by Mrs Sarah Marriott. Several generations of the

The Rochdale Pioneers Museum in Toad Lane.

Marriotts seem to have run the pub. A directory of 1798 shows her as the licensee of the 'Old' Roebuck, giving some confirmation of the tenancy of the Marriotts. The site of this 'Old' Roebuck is now occupied by Barclay's Bank.

The 'Old' Roebuck was decorated with a large gilded sign, no doubt recalling the history of hunting in the huge Rossendale Forest; another example is the Deerplay at Weir, near Bacup (see pp. 152–4) As a central pub in Rochdale, the 'Old' Roebuck would have provided a change of horses for coaches that connected destinations across the Pennines. Old sketches show the traditional archway leading into the courtyard where the stables were. In 1790 a 'market' coach ran from the Roebuck to Manchester.

Among the well-known personalities who stayed at the 'Old' Roebuck was the King of Denmark; he slept there on 1 September 1768. A written record of that visit is on the wall of the present Roebuck and lists the King's large retinue and the number of servants who attended them.

And the 'New' Roebuck? So flexible is our language that 'New' can mean what we want it to mean – a source of wonder to people elsewhere in the world. In Rochdale the building of what is now the Roebuck took place as far back as 1660, the year that Charles II was restored to the throne of England. The site was then called the Market Place, now Newgate.

There is some uncertainty about the exact date of the 'New' Roebuck's first licence and its opening. What we do know is that a Thomas Wordsworth was listed in the 1798 directory as being at the 'New' Roebuck and Excise Office. He died in 1800, so we can conclude that the licence had been transferred to the new pub some time at the turn of the century.

The 'New' Roebuck did much the same sort of business as its predecessor, including acting as a coaching and a posting house. Only a few yards from the 'Old' Roebuck's position, it could take over its role very easily. The Liberal Party made it its headquarters for elections; intimidation and violence at election times in the nineteenth century were common and there are several stories of fights on the premises.

Mention has already been made of Rochdale Town Hall, little more than a stone's throw away from the Roebuck. It is one of the finest Victorian town halls in the country, reflecting the powerful self-confidence of Rochdale's nineteenth-century leaders. It has outstanding stained glass, ceramics and carvings. It should not be missed and guided tours are available.

Few people are unaware that the Co-operative Movement began at Rochdale. The Rochdale Pioneers Museum in Toad Lane is a very short walk from the Roebuck: just follow the line of the pedestrian precinct past the shopping centre and turn left down the Baum. The Museum is across the road to the left. The displays explain the establishment of the first Co-operative Society in 1844 with a policy of offering fair value for a fair price.

ROUGHLEE
THE BAY HORSE INN and THE PENDLE WITCHES

M61 to J9, then M65 to J13. At Barrowford take A682 north.
On hill out of town look for signs at Blacko to Roughlee on the left (Blacko Tower is on the right); or M60 to J18, M66/A56 to M65, then as above.

To the casual visitor to the Bay Horse, the pub appears to be – as it says it is – just a traditional hostelry. In common with many, many others in the countryside, it was probably converted from a farmhouse, although its history is vague. But things are not always what they seem, as Roughlee is by no means just a destination for the casual visitor, but a fascinating village in its own right as well as a vital part of the Pendle Witches Scenic Car Trail.

The Bay Horse, Roughlee, an ideal spot to begin the Pendle Witches Scenic Car Trail.

Roughlee Old Hall.

Scenery there certainly is, with Pendle Hill dominating the skyline. Its vastness, its age and powerful presence have had an influence on people around it through the ages. Until recent times the Forest of Pendle was isolated, the people were poor and life was hazardous. Pagan beliefs in angry gods and folk tales to explain natural disasters were passed from one generation to the next, all part of life in the shadow of Pendle Hill. Even when Christianity had become well established elsewhere, many ancient beliefs still survived linked to the Pendle area with superstition having a formidable hold. There was also a strange preoccupation with supernatural powers.

The best way to appreciate the Pendle countryside and its ancient obsession with witchcraft is to visit first the Pendle Heritage Centre at Barrowford near Nelson. Whatever you decide to believe about the Pendle Witches, the scenery is unbeatable.

The Bay Horse at Roughlee stands facing the bridge over Pendle Water which feeds into the river Calder near Padiham. This has always been the centre of village life, and of employment too, as the Old Mill stood here, a substantial four-storey building of 1888 that had been rebuilt after a serious flood in 1881. In that year a 3-foot wall of water surged down Pendle Hill into Pendle Water, washing away bridges and whole sections of road; mills in the valley, including that at Roughlee, were seriously damaged. The Bay Horse suffered too, with beer barrels floating about in its flooded cellars.

After the First World War Roughlee had a population of about one thousand: there were thirty-six farms of various sizes that together with the cotton trade provided employment for the area. The Old Mill suffered the fate of many when economic conditions forced closures. If the mills at Burnley did not want the yarns spun at Roughlee, closure was inevitable sooner or later. It had come by 1909, when the Old Mill was listed as a laundry and bleachworks. During the 1940s it ceased production altogether. No longer was the massive water-wheel needed to power the machinery, neither was there an industrial use for the three million gallons of water in the Mill Lodge.

On the site of the Old Mill yard pleasure gardens were developed; the reservoir became a boating lake and a haven for fishermen. People came from far and wide at weekends to enjoy an afternoon at Roughlee; the Bay Horse was well placed to play its part. It is a stone-built house that has been extended on the right, as the stonework shows. The tables and chairs in the bar face the riverside frontage, while at the left-hand end a separate room is laid for formal meals. Today buses stop outside, bringing additional business, particularly in bad weather when it is a useful shelter.

Leaving the pub and going left, then left again at the next turning, a passage leads off to the right to Roughlee Old Hall, sometimes known as Witches Hall. This is a handsome Tudor house, once the home of Alice Nutter, who was hanged at Lancaster Castle as a witch. Now subdivided, it is a low two-storey house of local stone. It had a typical Tudor plan of a central hall and end wings, and was built by Miles Nutter. There was an inscribed stone at the south end, according to records over one hundred years ago; already almost illegible, it was thought to read 'This house was builded by M.N. in the year of Our Lord 1536'.

St Mary's Church at Newchurch-in-Pendle close by has a curious oval carving on the west side of the tower, taken to represent the 'Eye of God', giving protection against evil. To the right of the porch is the Nutter family grave, although Alice from Roughlee Old Hall is not buried there.

Pendle Hill.

St Mary's Church. The 'Eye of God' carving is below the clock.

The story of the witches is a tragic one, a consequence of the belief in villages around Pendle Hill of the existence of witchcraft. Had it not been for poverty and superstition there might not have been any accusations and trials. Once an eccentric homeless woman in the seventeenth century was seen to wander the district, begging, she became suspect; a refusal to give to her might result in a curse. It was not long before women like Demdike and Chattox (their witchcraft names) were living the part of witches; they may have had strange powers, but it was not until Demdike's granddaughter Alizon Devine was questioned by a magistrate that matters took a menacing turn. Alizon confessed, then accused her grandmother and Chattox of witchcraft, to which they both also confessed. All three, together with Anne Redfern, Chattox's daughter, were sent to Lancaster Castle, where Demdike died.

Malkin Tower, the home of Demdike and now lost, was the venue for a gathering of alleged witches on Good Friday 1612; it is said that the purpose was to plan to blow up Lancaster Castle and release the prisoners. When news of this reached the magistrate, more of the women were arrested and sent for trial, mainly on hearsay evidence.

Alice Nutter from Roughlee Old Hall was one of the nine found guilty and executed on 17 August 1612. She was different from the rest: a gentlewoman and practising Catholic. Her silence at her trial suggests that she might have been prepared to be found guilty of witchcraft rather than to implicate family and friends because of their Catholicism. These were, after all, intolerant times.

It is sometimes thought, quite wrongly, that Blacko Tower, which stands prominently on a hilltop above the A682 just north of Barrowford, is the Malkin Tower meeting-place of the witches. Although the meeting-place is likely to have been nearby, the tower seen today is a folly built in 1890 by Jonathan Stansfield to see further into Yorkshire – or is that yet another Pendle story?

Allow plenty of time to see more of Roughlee and to visit places that figure in accounts of the Pendle Witches. Roughlee's Bay Horse not only offers comfort and good food, but also has a convenient customers' car park.

A short walk upstream through the village is a pleasant way to see and hear the unexpected. Not far from the school, the quite placid Pendle Water drops deeply and dramatically over the weir, familiarly known as 'the waterfall' that provided water and power for the Old Mill. How important this was can be seen from documents of 1888 in which the then mill owner James Stuttard made representations about a Water Bill passing through Parliament at that time. He said that the weir turned the stream into a mill race which he had tunnelled through rock at great expense to take water to his reservoir. An accompanying map showed the line of the water channel into the pool, or Mill Lodge, which became a boating lake after the mill's closure. This great sheet of water some 2½ acres in extent is now a popular trout fishery business; all trace of the mill has gone and on its site are modern buildings, including the trout fishery premises. Down below by the bridge close to the Bay Horse is a large white house, formerly the home of the mill owner.

The waterfall at Roughlee.

Less than a mile away is Barley, with a picnic site and plenty of parking space with an information point. Not least, there are more spectacular views. There is no escaping Pendle Hill, its atmosphere and its mystery. George Fox climbed it in 1652 and his experiences on that day inspired him to found the Quakers. John Wesley visited Roughlee several times; on the first occasion he was chased out of the village and pelted with stones at Barrowford.

You can be assured of a more enjoyable welcome than that!

SAWLEY: *THE SPREAD EAGLE*

M6/M61 to J31, then A59; or M60 to J18, then M66, A56, cross M65, then A671/A59.

In the nature of things, most visitors to the Spread Eagle come via the A59 Preston road through Sawley village. In the spring they may well find it hard to believe the carpet of flowers on every grass verge. William Wordsworth had just the right words: 'A host of golden daffodils'.

Facing the corner of the Spread Eagle and pointing down the road that continues past the restaurant windows is a signpost that says:

Bolton by Bowland	2½
Wigglesworth	7½
Settle	12½

And running alongside the road is the river Ribble, wide and fast, with so many ducks that if it were not for the number of their supporters who come day after day to feed them, they would surely need to search far and near for food.

The Spread Eagle and, below, the glorious view from the dining room.

A short distance away down the Bolton by Bowland road is the arched bridge over the river (take care, the bends are fierce) and another signpost. Either choice here is a winner: Yorkshire-ward east, or westward to Grindleton, West Bradford, Waddington and the whole of the Ribble valley.

Back at the Spread Eagle, the two buildings that provide the front lounge and bar and the extension restaurant looking out on the river are first mentioned in seventeenth-century records, though they are considerably older. The Spread Eagle sign is, of course, an ancient one: the Romans used it, creating the imperial eagle as a symbol of power. It was also adopted by knights serving in war, especially overseas, such as during the Crusades.

The lounge and bar are particularly warm and welcoming. Among the easily recognisable drink labels on the pumps is a stranger that catches the eye. This says 'Sawley's Drunken Duck'; they are proud at the Spread Eagle to say that it is brewed specially for them at Bashall Eaves. They are even more proud of the food awards they have received: Lancashire's Dining Pub of the Year 2004 in the *Good Pub Guide* and Best Food Pub 2005 for Great Britain in the *Morning Advertiser*.

Blessed with the right facilities and in a beautiful location, the Spread Eagle is in demand for wedding receptions and anniversary meals as well as conferences, but the pub is still very much a family place and people travel long distances for a lunch visit or even for a coffee in front of the fire.

The remains of Sawley Abbey.

One of the fascinating possibilities is that the Spread Eagle is on what was once monastery land. Only a few yards away almost facing the pub is a huge arch that provides a gateway to a field. Do not be misled, as two such arches were once created from the ruins still remaining and set across the carriageway. They could not cope with modern traffic: the one survivor was rebuilt in its present role as a farm gateway. Other examples of abbey stonework can be seen in various places in Sawley village.

The monastery site is just a few steps from the rebuilt archway; it took its name Sawley (or Salley) Abbey from the willow trees or Sallows there. Its foundation in 1147 as part of the Cistercian Order was the work of a group of monks from Newminster Abbey in Northumberland who journeyed to Fountains in Yorkshire, thence to Ribblesdale. Unproductive soil and bad weather combined to make this a poor community; the buildings are small and few in number. Seen today, the ruins lack outer stone, which has been robbed for other purposes, leaving the church looking gaunt and insecure.

Sawley suffered the fate of other religious houses at the Dissolution of the Monasteries, but the monks were returned to Sawley when the Pilgrimage of Grace sought to oppose closures. When the protest failed the abbot was executed.

Come here and see history for yourself.

Slaidburn, near Clitheroe
Hark to Bounty Inn

M6 to J31, then A59/A671 to Clitheroe, then A6478 via Waddington and Newton; or M65 to J8, then A671 to Clitheroe, then A6478 as above.

Of all the villages in the Forest of Bowland, this is unforgettable. There are four routes into Slaidburn, each with its own special beauty. The journey south from Long Preston and Tosside is typical; it has fine views of Gisburn Forest and passes close to Stocks Reservoir, a haven for bird life, before the bridge over the river Hodder is crossed into the village. Just beyond the bridge, stone cottages face an attractive green with the river and open countryside in the distance.

This is good grazing country and it is no surprise that Slaidburn's name derives from 'a sheep field by a river'; close by, the river Hodder is joined by Croasdale Beck. A short walk from the river and car park up the narrow street past the war memorial leads to the crossroads that is a focal point of the village. Here is Hark to Bounty, with a shop and the former Black Bull, now a youth hostel, on opposite corners. Stone-built cottages crowd in along the roadside with a 'togetherness' feel; they are well cared for, just as the limestone walls bordering Bowland roads are immaculately kept.

The Hark to Bounty was known as the Dog until 1875; then it acquired its unusual name and reputation. At that date the village squire, who was also the parson (subsequently enjoying the curious title of squarson), made history. The Revd

Above: The river Hodder at Slaidburn is a haven for bird life. *Below:* External stairs lead to the ancient courtroom at the Hark to Bounty.

The former courtroom at the Hark to Bounty.

Henry Wigglesworth was Master of the Hunt, with a pack of hounds; one day out hunting he and his party called at the pub for refreshments. While they were drinking, their hounds outside were noisily demanding action. Loudest of all was the squire's favourite hound, which caused him to say 'Hark to Bounty'.

The hanging sign on the front of the pub illustrates the Hark to Bounty story; close to the sign are outside stone steps leading to an upper floor, a not unusual feature of a building dating from the thirteenth century. But in this case they were used for a most unusual purpose, as from about 1250 the upper floor was the courtroom of the Court of Bowland, an important centre for the administration of justice in the area. It was visited by travelling justices, being the only courtroom between York and Lancaster, and was still in use up to 1937. Its records remain in the county archives at Preston and at Clitheroe Castle.

Remarkably, much of the courtroom furniture, such as the high-backed oak benches, the dock and witness box, have survived. The room is enormous and stretches over the three downstairs lounge areas and the restaurant that seats sixty diners. Up to 120 people can be accommodated for functions in the courtroom and there are nine bedrooms with private facilities. Casual visitors are astonished to find that a modestly sized village pub is so extensive inside. Large numbers of guests from distant parts reflect the quality of the food and service, not least the popularity of a meal and drinks in front of a blazing open fire.

No matter which direction a walker takes from the Hark to Bounty, it gives pleasure and provides a camera opportunity. Perhaps the route taken by most visitors as a first venture at Slaidburn is signed to the Trough of Bowland, one of the most spectacular routes in Lancashire. Within the shortest of short walks is St Andrew's Parish Church; to see it at its best, go across to the south-west corner of the churchyard. The massive thirteenth-century tower is reputed to have provided protection to Slaidburn people during raids by the Scots in 1322 following their victory over the English at Bannockburn. The remainder of the church is fifteenth century and has a Norman font, a richly carved Jacobean rood screen and a three-decker pulpit.

Next door to St Andrew's Church is the fine Old Grammar School, mercifully preserved and still in use as the village primary school. Its Georgian façade is gracious and pleasing; its pedigree evidenced by an inscribed stone that records its foundation in May 1717. The cost of this superb building was borne by John Brennand, a local farmer.

The road past the church and school continues to Newton and Dunsop Bridge; for visitors intending to go on to the Trough of Bowland, this is the way. But do not leave Slaidburn too readily: it is a gem of history.

STALYBRIDGE, GREATER MANCHESTER: THE STATION BUFFET

By rail, 8 miles east of Manchester towards Huddersfield.
By road from Manchester area, M60 to J23 then A635 and A6018.

Anyone who has not heard of the Station Buffet need not feel guilty, because the souvenir glasses sold in the bar call it 'The pub that time forgot'. The first limited rail service to and from Stalybridge began at Christmas 1845, afterwards being extended through the Standedge Tunnel to Huddersfield.

Platform 1 at Stalybridge houses the Station Buffet. Seats outside provide fine views over the Pennines and close contact with all the activity when trains arrive.

It seems clear that the line was well used, but that Stalybridge station was quite inadequate; a new station was duly opened in 1885, when the buffet bar and its conservatory came into being. This Victorian masterpiece began to decline as rail travel became less popular in the twentieth century; in the 1990s it was closed and rapidly became derelict. Even the windows were shattered. A brave heart was needed to imagine a future for it, particularly as the sole remaining decision seemed to be a date for its demolition. Fortunately a record 15,000-name petition and campaign organised by CAMRA secured its survival; there are only two others of this age and style in the country.

What is it about Stalybridge that made this happen? The town is now in the district of Tameside, part of

The clock on Platform 1 with the buffet bar sign below.

Greater Manchester; like Ashton-under-Lyne, very much an industrial town. In spite of this, the sweeping view from the station platform is of the great Pennine Hills rising up close by over the roofs of the town.

Stalybridge cannot be one of the greatest visitor attractions in the world, but today's Station Buffet has its regulars and its train passengers (it is a junction for Manchester Piccadilly or Victoria), as well as its party goers – yes, party goers! Retirements, for example, are celebrated here, there is folk music on Saturday nights; on the second Wednesday evening of the month there is a Laurel and Hardy film, and beer festivals from time to time.

The place was transformed in all sorts of ways. From the reopening in 1996 under the present management, using the conservatory facing up Platform 1 and the bar, successive rooms, including the Station Master's Room with its decorated ceiling, have been brought into use. Today sixty to eighty people can enjoy a party evening.

Most of the fittings going back to 1885 have been preserved, and awards for the standard of refurbishment include one in 1998 from CAMRA's English Heritage Design. The Manchester Civic Society also made a Design Award in 1999 with a 'Highly Commended' grading.

On warm days platform tables and seats offer scenic views with the added excitement of a stopping train travelling east to Scarborough or Liverpool Lime Street going west; a through express can even halt conversation briefly. When Pennine winter weather comes the regulars do not hesitate; with a welcoming open fire, newspapers to read and a guest beer to sample, why freeze?

The length of the list of guest beers is remarkable; a constantly updated notice behind the marble-topped bar gives the number. On 31 March 2006 the figure since January 1997 stood at 5,872. Is this a record? Behind the bar is a long row of overseas beers – something for everyone's taste. Shaw's Brewery of Dukinfield has many supporters among the regulars: from the guest list Spellbinder seems to be one of the favourites.

Food orders here are substantial. If you want a reminder of the good old days you may like to try a pie (of various kinds) and mushy peas. For the real connoisseur there is the Buffet's black pea supper, which is famous. Not black, really, more a dark brown in colour, the peas are well soaked, dressed with salt and vinegar and eaten from a cup with a spoon. All for 50p.

The atmosphere of the past is all around: photographs of the station and the buffet as they used to be with steam-headed trains on the move. A reminder of the sound and of the smell of smoke. Did those locomotives ever break down? Signal arms and station signs make wonderful bar decoration, as they do at the Head of Steam at Huddersfield (see *Yorkshire's Historic Pubs*).

At one time there was a regular train service between Stockport and Stalybridge, which later became uneconomic. To close the line entirely involved a long, costly process, so a typical British solution was found: run one train a week. This was on Fridays, departing Stockport at 3.00 p.m. and covering the 12 miles in about twenty minutes. Even more peculiar: it didn't come back! It became known as the 'Ghost Train' and so caught the imagination of the editor of the *Saga Magazine* that in August 2000 he published a fictional account of the experiences of a group of passengers travelling on it.

By no means ghostly and certainly not fictional is the story of Fred Wood, recorded on a blue plaque outside the Stalybridge Buffet. Fred was a signalman from Stalybridge on duty at Dukinfield West box one day in 1909 when over fifty laden wagons broke away from a goods train, and careered loose towards another train packed with passengers approaching Stalybridge station.

Fred's quick thinking in switching the points and diverting the runaway saved countless lives. The scale of the tragedy he averted became clear when the wagons finally hit the buffers at the end of the line and literally took to the air. Nobody was hurt, and Fred was awarded a medal by the railway company.

An eastbound train arrives on Platform 1. Standing guard is the clock outside the buffet bar.

As a firm recommendation, take the train when visiting the Buffet. Travelling from the east, the Colne valley scenery is spectacular; near Marsden the train plunges into the Standedge Tunnel, emerging 3½ miles later on the Lancashire side. Only a few minutes to go before having the pleasure of the Stalybridge Station Buffet. Long may it remain.

WADDINGTON: *THE LOWER BUCK INN*

M6 to J31, A59 east, then A671 to Clitheroe; or M66, A56, cross M65 at J8, then A671 to Clitheroe. From Clitheroe take B6478 across Brungerley Bridge.

Originally the Roebuck Inn, the pub was built in 1760 and had a 33-acre farm to supplement the landlord's income. It was sold by the Parker family from nearby Browsholme (pronounced Brusom) Hall to the Waddington Hospital trustees for £3,000. The Hospital's annual Founder's Day celebration involved a church service; dinner at the Roebuck followed this. There was also a dinner given to tenants when they paid their half-yearly rents. Vestry and charity meetings and social events were held at the pub too.

Oddly, there was another pub in Waddington with a similar name to the Roebuck; this was the Buck i' th' Vine, which was located in the centre of the village. By 1864 it had become the Higher Buck; the Roebuck was usually known by that date as the Lower Buck, thus avoiding confusion.

Once a coaching inn, the Lower Buck's former coach house to the left of the building is now the landlord's house; the former stables are used as a garage and there was a barn across the road. It is very traditional, welcoming children and providing a family room across the passage from the bar; behind the bar is a room where a number of regulars meet. There is no music and no electronic games.

There were three regulars at the bar that April lunchtime. A fragment of their conversation floated across: 'I remember when . . .'. So it was nostalgia day, anticipating the village May Day celebration the following weekend. There was to be a May Day Queen, the world-famous Duck Race and a Scarecrow Festival; entries of scarecrows were being invited by a life-size model of Hyacinth Bouquet (or Bucket) in the church lych gate holding a basket of flowers and an invitation card.

Waddington is that sort of village where people have always taken part, depending on each other for entertainment and making a contribution to a successful community. Social needs in the past made Waddington self-sufficient: there were shops, of course, builders, joiners and wheelwrights, shoe and clog makers and farm workers.

Waddngton: any moment now the door will open.

The bar at the Lower Buck just opened for the day.

Away from their work, people's social needs were met through participation in the activities of numerous organisations: there was the Ancient Order of Foresters, the Brass Band, the Hand Bell Ringers, the Sunday Schools and their Whit Monday procession and sports teams.

But work on farms and estates, as well as in the old domestic textile occupations, could not survive. The sixteen farms that existed before the Second World War have shrunk to two today; in the nineteenth century twenty-nine men were listed as handloom weavers, while many women spun wool or flax as well as raising a family. Factory production changed all that: Garnetts at Low Moor had 1,200 spindles powered by water, as was the case on a smaller scale at Feizor cotton mill at Waddington. Both are long since gone.

Such were the changes, yet a member of a Waddington family could emigrate, not return for many years, then return to the Square and find it much the same. So much depended on the support

'Hyacinth' invites you . . .

given to the village by leading families such as the Parkers of Browsholme. It was Robert Parker who founded and endowed Waddington Hospital in the seventeenth century; trustees were appointed in 1701 and it is to them that the Lower Buck pays rent. The lovely quadrangle of almshouses is just at the turn of the road out of the village towards West Bradford.

Waddington Old Hall, which faces the attractive Elizabeth II Coronation Gardens along Waddington Brook, played a crucial part in history. After the defeat of the Lancastrian army at Hexham in 1464, Henry VI was secretly hidden at the Hall. It was the Talbots of Bashall who learned that the King was there and sought his capture; he escaped, only to be caught trying to cross the river, and was detained in the Tower of London in 1461.

It is entirely natural that Waddington should win Best Kept Village competitions, such is the care that the villagers take of their homes and community. What is not unusual is not that Waddington won the award for Yorkshire (yes – Yorkshire) in 1966, but that since the boundary change of 1974 it has won the title for Lancashire. Is this a record?

Clearly this is 'border' country; it used to have advantages, if pub tales are to be believed. The official pub closing time in Clitheroe was thirty minutes earlier than in Waddington, so the bars at Clitheroe began to empty swiftly towards closing time as the mass exit to Waddington started, to take advantage of a half-hour's extra

Many visitors go to Waddington just to see the Coronation Gardens.

drinking time. There's more! When the Lower Buck's last orders were taken the front bar closed and everyone retreated to the back, where activities continued as usual. Someone said 'until the early hours'. Perhaps a very long time ago, but it suggests that the long arm of the law did not reach to Waddington – unless it was just another bar tale.

There were wonderful village characters too. Their tales and gossip would have enlivened many an evening at the Old Buck. The landlord produced a copy of a recent Waddington parish magazine with an article entitled 'Old Waddington' written over the name of 'Old Bowland'. Everyone knows who he is, of course. Most of the article concerns nicknames, including a colourful account of life in the village before flush toilets when the emptying wagon was called 'Sweet Violet'. Those were the days!

WARTON: *THE GEORGE WASHINGTON INN*

From Preston, M6 to J35, then A601(M) to J35a, A6 north. Turn left on Threagill Lane to Warton Main Street.

If you go a couple of miles further north you are in Cumbria, so Warton is the 'turn-round' point in this collection of Lancashire pubs. But it is a turn-round with a flourish: visit Warton on 4 July and you will see the Stars and Stripes flying from the tower of St Oswald's Church in honour of American Independence Day.

They say in Warton that the Stars and Stripes were on this church tower flag before they were adopted for the national flag of the United States of America. George Washington's ancestors (eighteen members of the family) were important members of the community at Warton and helped to build the fifteenth-century church. The Washington family coat of arms, which carried three stars and two bars, must surely have been the inspiration for the American flag, or so it is strongly argued at Warton.

Only a few steps along Main Street from the church is the George Washington pub; could it have had any other name? One of the guides at the Carnforth Station Visitor Centre (pp. 37–9) who, of course, comes from Warton, insisted that it be included in this book. Very sound advice!

Apart from a well-painted President Washington pub sign outside, the pub's interior has paintings, prints and etchings of George Washington wherever you look, including a fine family portrait. If you show the slightest interest in them, a regular will be sure to point out one particular painting of the great man looking in one direction that also has the face of a lady facing the opposite way, and only visible from one angle and distance. Perhaps a mistress, you will be told, rather doubtfully.

In pride of place is a fine English flintlock pistol of the eighteenth century and said to have been a favourite of General Washington. The history of the Washingtons and their family tree are well displayed, as are records of legal matters such as tenancy agreements and brushes with the law.

Although the Washingtons do not seem to have been directly involved in it, there is a well-preserved copy of Warton's Market Charter dated 1200 and witnessed by the Bishops of London and Winchester. It is an ancient township – perhaps better defined today as a village. The pub's own history is plainly displayed: 'This building was here when Robinson Crusoe and Moll Flanders books were written by Daniel Defoe 1660–1731.'

The whole of the front area of the pub to left and right of the bar is an open space, with a smaller dining room to the rear. Darts are played at one end of the bar, with the trophies won at the other. The English Tourist Council gave the pub a Three Diamond award for its guest accommodation in 1999.

A framed quotation by Dr Johnson on the wall is entitled 'Tribute to pubs' and runs, 'There is nothing which has yet been contrived by man, by which so much happiness is produced as by a good tavern or inn.'

The notice continues 'Where, after all, do charities go first to hang little net Christmas stockings, money boxes and appeals for everything from children to deaf aids for tired dogs? To a bar, sir. The point of view is that men who like pubs are less mean in the mind, less pinched in the soul, than those who don't.'

At Warton the George Washington is a valuable refreshment stop before reaching the county border into Cumbria.

The landlord in the bar at the George Washington and the best source of information in the district.

As you would expect, there is a strong Washington family connection with St Oswald's Church; they were baptised there and the last Washington to live at Warton was Thomas Washington, vicar from 1799 to 1823. He is buried in the churchyard and his headstone is against the wall at the east end of the church.

Behind and overlooking the pub and the village is Warton Crag; beyond to the north is the Leighton Moss Nature Reserve with an interesting variety of habitats, including the largest reedbed in north-west England. Wildlife includes rare birds such as bittern, bearded tits and marsh harriers, as well as mammals such as roe and red deer.

Very close to the Nature Reserve is Leighton Hall, set against the background of the Lakeland fells, its pale limestone gleaming in the sun. Given a neo-Gothic treatment in the early 1800s, it replaced a rather plain classical style. It was sold to Richard Gillow in 1822, the grandson of Robert Gillow, founder of the famous Lancaster firm of furniture makers.

Thomas Washington's headstone in the churchyard at Warton. He was once vicar there.

This is a charming house, open to the public, with an outstanding collection of Gillow furniture. There are fine gardens, too; the sweet peas there are, as they say, 'out of this world'.

WEIR, NEAR BACUP: *THE DEERPLAY*

A671 Bacup to Burnley beyond Weir village.

It was one of those days in February that started well; decent enough until mist began to gather. The higher the road climbed the thicker it became until on the Burnley road above Weir a notice that the Deerplay was but 100 yards further was quite a relief.

No outdoor photography for sure, but the great consolation was the pub's food and fire. A notice said 'Order at the kitchen' – excellent advice, especially if you enjoy steak and kidney pie. It was superb: a good reason for a return visit. Was photography just an excuse?

This is empty country and at a height of 1,326 feet the Deerplay is a reminder of the Tan Hill Inn in Yorkshire and the Cat and Fiddle in Derbyshire. Like them, it has to be prepared for snow in mid-winter; a photograph in the bar shows a car stranded in the snow. Behind the pub, which faces downhill, the skyline is dominated by Thievely Pike; below is the expanse of Deerplay Moor from which the pub takes its

The lonely Deerplay high up between Bacup and Burnley.

Unusual cloud effects – perhaps jet trails – above the war memorial close to Thievely Pike.

unique name. When the Forest of Rossendale really was a forest the richness of its wildlife brought the deer hunters.

The original Deerplay stood on the opposite side of the Burnley road; when it was demolished some 200 years ago two cottages were converted into the present, or 'new' Deerplay. The entrance door leads into the end cottage with the small bar modestly, even coyly, sheltering in the roadside corner of the spacious lounge. Leading off it, close to a large open fireplace (prepare to shed two layers), crowned by a brass stag's head, are two open dining areas, with the kitchen at the end of the building.

In the dining area are many photographs of the Deerplay over the generations; there is a strong sense of its isolation and of its witness to affairs beyond the law. A framed document headed 'Notice to the people' reports in some detail the execution of Dick Turpin at York on 7 April 1739. No doubt a warning to all.

Below is a copy of an article from the *Lancashire Evening Telegraph* of Wednesday 6 April 1988, headed 'Where Dick Turpin drank'. The author does not claim that Dick Turpin was a regular at the Deerplay itself, along the familiar lines of 'Queen Elizabeth slept here', but maintains that he had relatives who lived here and he visited them several times. It does, of course, explain the 'Notice to the people'.

The Deerplay's painted sign is a handsome one; located at the corner of the car park, it has a background of a distant row of cottages down the hill, the first trace of a community for miles en route from Burnley to Bacup. Otherwise scattered farmhouses are the pub's only near neighbours along the A671; opposite the Deerplay the old walled turnpike – even lonelier – branches off downhill towards Bacup.

On the walls of the bar are maps of long and challenging walks that groups have attempted in the locality; for the less energetic there is plenty to enjoy close at hand.

Still with the winter snow around, a little stream later to become the river Irwell runs behind the Deerplay.

Fortunately a paved path along the roadside provides safe walking and makes possible an expedition to see the hilltop war memorial close to Thievely Pike, leaving the car in the car park.

The footpath leading up to the Pike passes close to reedy, spongy ground that can only be the result of water draining down from the hillsides. Springs here include the source of the river Irwell, once polluted along its whole length to Manchester and beyond from the factories that developed on its banks during the Industrial Revolution. Looking at the clear water at its source, it seems unbelievable today and it is possible to see it now, trickling fresh and clear behind the Deerplay before running downhill into Bacup, where it is recognisably a flowing river.

WHEELTON
THE DRESSERS ARMS and
THE VILLAGE WITHOUT A PUB

M6/M60 to M61, J8. Take A674 Blackburn road. In about 2 miles at sign on right for Brinscall. Pub on left.

For a pub to succeed – handsomely – when so many landlords are saying 'time' for the last time and closing their doors for good, there must be compelling reasons, especially when it is out of town and regulars have to make a real effort, rain or shine, to fill their customary places at the bar.

The Dressers Arms is on the 'wrong side' of the A674 Chorley–Blackburn road which bypassed Wheelton village in 1966, yet still they come. One regular in particular is remembered with affection: Big Frank had his own corner at the Dressers until, sadly, he went to the local in the sky. His place at the bar, perhaps his piece of the bar, was duly marked with a brass plate which reads 'Big Frank's Corner. Fond memory of our mate Kingsley Frank Moyle'.

There were also those who wanted to remember Frank, particularly when they raised their glasses, and there is a special beer pump at the bar which is labelled 'Big Frank's Bitter': the popularity of this smooth, fruity bitter is a credit to the brewer, the pub landlord, and – of course – to Frank. Ask for a sample drink: even if bitter is not normally for you, have one in memory of Frank.

The pub's reason for being there at all was first and foremost to provide somewhere for the men from the quarry further up the Brinscall road to quench their thirst after a day's heavy work. The pub is just below the access road to Slate Delph and the men were employed there as slate dressers, although the so-called slates were really pieces of stone. There are photographs all round the bar showing

Dining in the attractive garden of the Dressers Arms makes a visit there an especially pleasant experience.

The Dressers Arms once had its own tiny brewery, now just an extension to the dining area.

different operations at the quarry and there is no doubt that it was hard, exhausting work, in all weathers.

With a limited clientele of that kind, the Dressers Arms is likely to have been at first a farm combined with an ale-house brewing its own beer and going back perhaps 400 years. Until well after the Second World War it was the smallest pub in Lancashire: just one room and a stillage. Until recently the room served as a micro-brewery, now off the premises, and is a dining area.

Fortunately the next-door cottages owned by the quarry company became available and have been added to the original building, making it a substantial pub with real character. The cottage rooms vary greatly in size, are furnished in keeping and have their fireplaces and low-beamed ceilings as always. Character is preserved and the old tradition survives; the step down into the games room is a huge stone that would have supported the whole house. Unfortunately the deeds of the Dressers Arms only show the landlords as far back as 1802, but it is likely that before that date farming was the main occupation and the occupier would have been recorded as a farmer; pub work would have been a secondary occupation.

Such has been the change since 1802, including a separate and recent Cantonese restaurant upstairs, that the old quarrymen would be astonished to see the pub today. What would they think of diners having their meals outside under coloured umbrellas? The large car park across the road is ample evidence of the popularity of the Dressers Arms and of the quality of its food and drink.

One odd remnant of the past can be seen in the names of roads at Wheelton. The Dressers Arms stands on Briars Brow (sometimes Briers Brow), which is believed to have been Friars Brow – or Friary Hill, from the Friary once there. Further along off Harbour Lane a track goes to Munshill, more correctly Monks Hill. Wheelton itself was a cotton village; handloom weaving was a domestic occupation, replaced by mill work after the Industrial Revolution.

The village without a pub: Withnell Fold

This is a treasure to wonder at – if you know where to look. Continue along the A674 towards Blackburn through Higher Wheelton and look for a stone bus shelter on the left; just beyond is a sign for Withnell Fold fixed to a wall. Soon the tarmac surface is replaced by setts and a 20 mph zone starts, so – gently does it! One remaining chimney from this former industrial village and a delightful square of estate cottages greet a visitor. Parking is allowed on the green 'at the discretion of the residents' – what a gracious touch!

It all began when the Parke family opened a paper mill in 1844 near Withnell Fold Farm and built cottages to accommodate their workers. The Parkes had already made a good deal of money from cotton, so they were able and anxious to develop a model village round the mill. This included a chapel, a reading room and other social facilities, but no pub. The family were Methodists and believed in teetotalism. Where the workers went to drink can only be guesswork: there is a pub in Higher Wheelton and, of course, there was the Dressers Arms.

There is still no pub in Withnell Fold, but the Reading Room is now a private house and a number of modern houses have been built up the hill towards the

Rural richness: the canal at Withnell Fold with the old mill chimney peeping up over the trees.

Now very much a family home, this is the former Reading Room in the Parkes' model village.

Just by the gate of the village primary school is this fascinating tree carving. You can park close by, as always, at residents' discretion. Admire their gardens and you will have no problem.

Blackburn road. The paper mill closed in the 1960s; much has been demolished, but one mill building is used by several small industrial businesses. The place the Parkes used was well chosen, close to the Leeds & Liverpool Canal at Bridge No. 88, where their raw materials were unloaded.

Walk the few steps down to the bridge; the towpath is well maintained, there are good views and a fine nature reserve has been developed close by around old disused filter beds. It is an attractive place just to lean on the bridge and contemplate the past. On the way back to the car (at residents' discretion!) look for the village stocks facing the car park and admire the tree carving outside the village primary school.

WHITEFIELD (OR PRESTWICH)
THE COACH & HORSES

M60 to J17, turn north on A56. At junction with A665 (lights) turn right. Pass under railway bridge on Bury Old Road. Pub on the right.

Perhaps one of these days some student will choose the address of the Coach & Horses as the subject of their dissertation. Local sensitivities always cloud issues like this, although to the traveller the real question is: how easily can I find my destination? Here it is so easy with the motorway nearby that legal and political niceties are best ignored.

A very urban setting for the Coach & Horses. Road traffic seems to surround it and the railway is only yards away.

The friendly bar at the Coach & Horses.

The Coach & Horses' name and handsome sign are reminders of how important highways and travel have been and how many pubs have adopted names as a result. Until turnpike trusts began to improve roads, coach services could not develop and it was not until 1754 that a coach made regular journeys from Manchester to London; this took four and a half days.

Hundreds of Coach & Horses pub signs appeared as the years passed, as well as others of a similar kind such as the Mail Coach and Coach and Six. The sign 'Rest and be thankful' used by a pub on a coach route must have been at the end of a particularly long and unpleasant stage. It is believed that the Coach & Horses on Bury Old Road was built in 1830; it would be surprising if there had not been an earlier pub on the site, or close by. Today the traffic streams past, nose to tail at peak times and, within earshot, the M60 vehicles hurtle along, all going somewhere in a hurry.

Occasionally a train can be heard, too. Besses o' th' Barn station is only yards away, with the rail bridge crossing Bury Old Road. Once train services became widely available it was feared it would be the end of pubs like the Coach & Horses, but many survived because they became a focal point for the community: a meeting-place for everyone. Where else would there be someone who cared enough to go to collect and guide to the pub a regular whose sight was failing and who could no longer cross busy roads safely?

The Coach & Horses is not ancient – not even very old – unless you are in an age group that thinks 1830 is very old. Its records show that it served the Manchester to

Burnley coaches. The pleasant garden at the rear, just right for summer evenings, is quite private; it would have been the turn-around for coaches in the nineteenth century and the courtyard entrance remains, even though the stables have long since gone.

Inside little has changed: the bar at the end of the entrance hall and the three rooms to left and right still attract their own particular regulars who would not think of sitting anywhere else. The lounge has had a bay window added, but give or take a few changes of wallpaper the Coach & Horses is 'as was'. The Tap Room (the Vault) and the Snug (once the Bar Parlour) are conversational rooms; even a stranger with a camera quickly becomes one of the party. The Tap Room is for the sporty types, as it is lined with photographs of boxers in action and racing drivers – just the place for a re-run on Saturday evenings of the afternoon home match. The Snug is more classical; it has the notices of the Coach & Horses Golf Society's doings and a display of prints of Van Gogh's self-portraits. The Golf Society was founded in 1997 and is still going strong.

In the bar entrance are a number of photographs of old Whitefield – at least their titles do not mention Prestwich or any other place-name. Bury New Road with trams is a favourite subject and Whitefield station with an old-fashioned signal shows a train is due. Past photographs have a special fascination and often prompt people to reminisce; at such times treasures of memory come to light. Bury Old Road past the Coach & Horses was very likely the route of the Roman road that ran south from Ribchester to Manchester (see Ribchester, the White Bull, pp. 124–8). Would that we knew more about that road!

Christie's Hospital is a household word not only in Manchester, but nationally too and there is a special connection with the Coach & Horses, which is a Holt's Brewery pub. Since the days of Joseph Holt the Brewery has supported the work done by the Hospital; even today every pint of beer sold at the Coach & Horses attracts a penny to Christie's from the Brewery. Multiplied by the number of Holt's pints sold, that is generosity indeed, supporting an outstanding service.

Without a caring landlord the collection for Christie's would never happen, neither would a regular losing his sight be brought for a drink. At the Coach & Horses he really means it when he says 'No problem'; for him it is not just a form of words like 'Have a nice day'.

All the many attractions of Manchester are within easy reach of a visitor to the Coach & Horses, but there is something special close enough to be 'in the neighbourhood'. That is All Saints' Church at Stand on the Whitefield side of the M60 and close to the extension of Bury Old Road, A665, when it becomes Higher Lane. Built at much the same time as the Coach & Horses, it was designed by Sir Charles Barry, who built the Palace of Westminster after the fire of 1834.

All Saints' is in the Gothic Revival style; its height and high position make it visible from a long way off. If you enjoy decorative stonework and stained glass, you should not miss the church and the work of a master architect.

WHITEWELL, FOREST OF BOWLAND
THE INN AT WHITEWELL

From Preston, B6243 via Elston, Grimsargh and Hurst Green. At Great Mitton turn north and follow signs to Bashall Eaves and Browsholme Hall to Whitewell. From Clitheroe cross Edisford Bridge towards the Trough of Bowland. Follow signs to Bashall Eaves and Browsholme Hall to Whitwell.

Picture a heavily wooded valley, glimpses of the river far below and suddenly out of nowhere a little church and a country inn. No – not part of the itinerary of a coach tour in Switzerland or Austria – just a car ride in the Bowland Forest of Lancashire. Any further north and you would be in the Trough of Bowland, one of the unforgettable routes in Lancashire; to the south the softer open country that surrounds the river Ribble.

This particular day was dull and wet, the Inn at Whitewell was busy, people were waiting for tables for lunch, yet the welcome at the bar was just as warm as at any desirable restaurant. The assistant at the bar said 'Good morning, young man' and the waitress brought me my fish pie promptly and served it with a wonderful smile: the two of them changed my day.

The experience of a visit to the inn, or a stay in one of their seventeen bedrooms, gives an opportunity to enjoy the pub as it is today and to appreciate the place as it was in local history.

The Inn at Whitewell, as handsome now as it was in medieval times when it was a manor house.

A new window at the Inn at Whitewell opens to a delightful view.

The main dining areas and a bar with log fires have country-style furniture, real beams and mullioned windows. Family-size tables bring many family groups in to eat and offer strangers a chance to meet and talk over a meal. One commentator described the atmosphere here as 'shabby grandeur', which does not do it justice, as its comfort arises from its countryside past which they have carefully retained. It would be disastrous if that were lost in order to modernise. Why try, when the food and drink are superb and the views are unbelievable?

The history of the pub goes back to the days when the building was the manor house of Walter Urswyck, Keeper of the Royal Forest of Bowland. He established a chapel close by in about 1400, both buildings having alterations and repairs in 1422.

Walter Urswyck's manor house, now the Inn at Whitewell, still has some of the early fifteenth-century building within its fabric. In past days the Swaincote and Woodmote Courts met here; the Bowland Forest tenants would come and give accounts of their activities to the Master Forester and Keepers. This was deer country and the maintenance of deer enclosures was a serious responsibility. While hunting deer is now very much a matter of history, fishing remains an important leisure activity; those looking for an activity holiday need look no further, as the inn has 6 miles of salmon- and trout-fishing rights.

Seen from the Inn car park, the present, rebuilt church is on the left of the pub. It dates from 1818 and is dedicated to St Michael. Originally a thatched Chapel of Ease, it provided a resting place for bodies en route to burial at a consecrated church elsewhere. It still has a fifteenth-century window, in spite of its rebuilding, a fine Jacobean pulpit and a very beautiful tapestry based on Rubens's *Descent of Jesus from the Cross* at Antwerp Cathedral.

In the account of Waddington, the Lower Buck (see pp. 145–9), there was a brief reference to the Parker family of Browsholme Hall. The Hall is close to Whitewell

Every turn of the road along the Trough of Bowland has views like this. No wonder it is so popular.

and is of such beauty and interest that no visitor to the Inn should miss the opportunity to go to Browsholme.

The Parker family, Bowbearers of the Forest of Bowland, have lived at Browsholme since 1507. Set in a landscaped park in the style of Capability Brown, the Hall is still very much a family home for the three generations who still live there.

In 1604 the house was refaced with red sandstone. This, together with the pillared entrance and central windows, added a warm, decorative feature formerly lacking. The hall has a remarkable antiquarian collection with paintings by masters such as Devis, Romney and Batoni, superb oak and Regency furniture, porcelain, armour and embroidered waistcoats.

If you do not have time to drive along at least part of the Trough of Bowland, do go a mile north from the Inn as far as Burholme Bridge. On the north side of the bridge is a comfortable turn-round area; the river and hill views towards the Trough will surely bring you back again soon to Whitewell.

WIGAN
THE SWAN AND RAILWAY INN and THE ORWELL

By rail: to Wallgate and North West stations.
By road: M6 to J25, then A49; or M61 to J5, then A577.

When you visit Wigan take a good appetite with you, because you will be in the 'Land of the Loaded Barmcake'. Just in case you think it is probably just another bap, or a teacake, or perhaps a flourcake with a filling, stop, think again and

The imposing exterior of the Swan and Railway.

ponder on the following menu entry: 'Two sausages, two bacon and two eggs on a Bin Lid Barmcake'. Now that is loaded!

The importance of the Wigan you see today can be judged from the early date of its charter as a borough: 26 August 1246. It was then of equal status with Lancaster, Liverpool and Preston, and much more important than Manchester; once a chartered market had been granted, Wigan's future was assured. Because of its manufacturing resources, especially coal, Wigan was bound to become a vital part of the future canal network; one of the first railways in the country was built here in 1831 as a branch of the Liverpool and Manchester railway.

The Swan and Railway Inn

No wonder, then, that the pub in Wallgate known as the Swan in the early 1800s should later become the Swan and Railway. It stands almost next door to Wigan Wallgate station, with the North West station just across the road and the bus station only a few steps further away. Getting to the Swan and Railway by public transport could not be easier.

In its early days the Swan (and Railway) was owned by Walkers' Brewery of Warrington, having been bought by them from a private owner in the early 1900s. It was in the Walkers' ownership longer than any pub in the town; listed in the Wigan Directory of 1909, Peter Jolly was named as the victualler.

There have been drastic changes from the records of the Swan in the early 1800s. The work of the architect W.E.V. Crompton in 1898 shows the influence of the Arts and Crafts Movement and art nouveau; outside, the rounded oriel windows and gable decoration above in terracotta are quite outstanding.

The locomotive plaque in the Swan and Railway. Count the number of kitchen utensils used to build it.

The huge nineteenth-century stained-glass panel in the bar of the Swan and Railway.

Inside, the floor of the entrance hall has the pub name in small mosaic tiles; three panels of moulded green floral tiles are on the wall just beyond the door. Look for the mistake by the tiler, who set one of the tiles the wrong way round.

The bar, which is back to back with the hall, is modest in size, but possesses an astonishing panel of stained glass more than 12 feet long showing a white swan at its centre and a railway locomotive in a panel at each end. Look carefully at the engine panels; you will see that they are American designs, with so-called 'cow catchers' on the front. It would have cost so much to have them replaced that they have been left as architectural disasters.

Over the door at the end of the bar is a plaque representing a locomotive. It is unique in that all the parts of the engine are made from kitchen utensils: the boiler is the round side of a cooking grater and the wheels were once clock faces. The designer even found a use for one of the old-style telephone dials. On the opposite wall is a collection of railway photographs and framed drawings of designs for old locomotives that must have great historic value.

A group of past railway workers calling themselves the 'Railway Children' meet at the pub every month and come from as far afield as Scotland. Their pride in their skill and experience and loyalty to the rail industry is matched by affection for the pub, perhaps deeper than one would expect. One of the group was responsible for the curious locomotive plaque over the door.

In the 1980s a fire gutted the pub, which was empty for three years; extensive rebuilding and refurbishment brought new life to the Swan and Railway. The new licensees had a policy for traditional ales and value-for-money meals, which has continued, together with a development of the hotel side of the business. There is a well-appointed games room and a restaurant that will seat more than fifty diners. As a local reporter wrote, using a well-turned phrase, 'The Swan and Railway is set to stay on the right track.'

The Orwell, Wigan Pier

To be the victim of a joke is hardly a pleasant experience, and Wiganers have had to live with the Wigan Pier joke since 1891, or so it seems. The story, recounted in documents in the library at the History Shop, is confirmed by John Hannavy in his *Wigan* (2003).

In the spring of 1891 a trainload of miners returning from a demonstration at Southport in support of an eight-hour working day was held up at signals on the edge of Wigan. The flooded countryside, with the elevated railway used for trans-porting coal to barges, resembled a seaside pier; along it, the engine house looked like the Promenade Pier at Southport. When one of the passengers asked the signalman where they were, the reply was 'Wigan Pier'.

Once established, the joke refused to go away; it was used over and over again by George Formby Senior on the music-hall stage. There was simply no chance of its being forgotten after the publication of George Orwell's *The Road to Wigan Pier*. Much earlier Jack Winstanley had given advice to Wiganers in his 'Ballad of Wigan Pier'. It begins:

> If you are told that there's a pier
> In Wigan town somewhere
> Don't laugh it off like others do,
> Look round you'll see it there
> It's spick and span and painted white
> And standin' out a mile
> But if you're asked just where it is
> Don't say much, just smile.

In the end, the people of Wigan realised that although it had become derelict, Wigan Pier (or Basin) was a huge asset if only they could exploit it. This the Wigan Civic Trust made possible with a extensive restoration programme in 1982.

The Orwell is one part of that restoration, which included the former warehouses, Trencherfield Mill and the waterfront. The Orwell is brick-built, comprising a pub and restaurant complex in a former warehouse dating from about 1880 when additional warehouse space was needed to cope with increasing business. All three floors are in use; day-to-day users dine on the ground floor, or have outside waterfront seating in warm weather. Upper floors are available for catering for special events and occasions, for which there are

The pub, named from George Orwell, and the museum at Wigan Pier.

A waterbus on its way back from a visit to Trencherfield Mill, seen in the background.

passenger lifts; there is a bar on each floor and the views across the whole site are remarkable.

The early use of the building is still to be seen, especially on the upper floors, where the equipment for hoisting heavy loads has been preserved. Panelling and a new wooden-lined roof have retained a Victorian flavour, while the separation of the ground floor into 'booths' provides the much-needed intimacy in such a large floor area. The Orwell has been the local CAMRA Pub of the Year twice.

Located as it is, close to 'The Way We Were' exhibition, the story of Wigan's past, the Orwell gives visitors an opportunity to see the exhibition and to take a waterbus tour that includes a stop at Trencherfield Mill. This once employed 1,000 people and was powered by the largest mill engine in the world, which is still operational. It generates 2,100 h.p. and has a 26-foot-diameter rope drum that used to supply power to all the floors of the mill.

Her Majesty the Queen opened the Pier officially in 1986 and it was that year when Robin Harston took over the Orwell and developed the pub into the highly successful establishment it has become.

WOODPLUMPTON: *THE PLOUGH AT EAVES*

From Preston, take A6 to Broughton, continue towards Barton. Turn left into Station Lane (opposite a phone box and a sign 'RC Church'). Cross railway and canal (hump-back bridge). At road junction keep left: pub on right.
From M6, J32, take M55. At J1 take A6 and follow above route.

The Plough is sometimes described, unfairly, as the most difficult pub to find in Lancashire – but is well worth seeking out; it is the oldest pub in the Fylde. None of its listed addresses seems particularly helpful; there is an Eaves Farm and an Eaves Lane (where the pub is located), but no village of Eaves. The Woodplumpton address leads into a network of lanes lacking signs at most of the junctions, so follow the directions as above: they are the strong recommendation of mine hosts at the Plough.

At one time the pub was called the Plough at Cuddy Hill, or the Cuddy Pub. Cuddy Hill represents an area rather than a village community, but it does have a claim to fame as the site of a battle in 1546, part of the endless conflict at that time between the English and the Scots. The Plough is believed to be somewhere on the battlefield, but the earliest record we have of a pub there is 1625. It was then a free house.

Once seen, the Plough is always remembered: it has a low silhouette, is painted white and is linked to a taller two-storey stone house that seems to be guarding the pub. A closer view reveals a truly magnificent hand-painted pub sign: a ploughman working with two great shire horses. It is worth a prize.

The side door, which seems to be the main entrance, leads into a long flagged corridor; immediately inside is a big painting, *Plough at Eaves*, in a heavy frame with a wooden chest below it. A dining area is on the left, the bar area at the end of the corridor. Low ceilings, heavy dark beams and horse brasses set the tone; with first-class cooking, including the Plough Whale, a massive piece of haddock in batter with chips and mushy peas, the pub has a deserved reputation. Ask anyone from Preston! Crowds collect quickly, especially at weekends, when it is wise to book a table.

Close as it is to the river Ribble and historic crossings, it is not surprising to find that there were other battles in the area. An ancient engraving in the Plough shows troops crossing the bridge at Walton le Dale as part of Cromwell's Civil War operations.

There are several other historic prints of interest: *The Last Days of Whalley Abbey*, with soldiers leading out the monks as the Abbey was closed at the Dissolution of

A profile easily remembered, with the stone house linked to the long, white, traditional pub building.

The village stocks outside the parish church at Woodplumpton.

the Monasteries, and *The Palmy Days of Hoghton Tower*. A light-hearted reproduction shows Preston Guild in the seventeenth century entitled *Old Fashioned Lancashire Holiday*.

The whole of the area beyond the bar and along the side of the pub next to the road is used for dining. Apart from visitors to the pub it is a quiet road, once a drovers' track, so sitting outside is a pleasure; to the rear, french windows open out on to grass and flowers. There is plenty of parking space and a large play area for children on the grass.

Imagine the consternation at the Plough one day when, dressed for the part, an Ale-taster arrived with fanfare to carry out his traditional duty as part of the regulation of the sale of ale that went back as far as the 1300s. Ale-house keepers were required to display a so-called ale stake as a sign that there was ale for sale and open to inspection.

The Ale-taster was always easily recognisable through his equipment and uniform: a pot for the ale and leather breeches to allow him to carry out the 'breeches test'; but to see him at the Plough – and at work – must have been a total surprise. He collected a little ale in his pot, poured some on to a wooden bench, sat on it

The boulder placed over Meg Shelton's grave at Woodplumpton to prevent her using her witch's powers to escape.

and after a short while rose to see whether or not his breeches had stuck to the seat. If so, by how much. He was able to tell from this whether the sugar content of the drink was satisfactory. Of course, the flavour was important too; hardly scientific, but there was a happy result for the Plough at Eaves, as he issued the following verdict:

Proclamation

The annual ceremony of Ale Tasting

This is to certify that on 9 October in the year of Our Lord 2003 ale in this hostelry has been found most palatable. From this day forward to be known as one of the finest in the realm.

There were a number of unpleasant penalties for innkeepers who failed the test or used false measures, ranging from a fine to a ducking in the village pond. Worst of all, if the ale was particularly bad, the innkeeper might be required to drink it all himself. There was never a danger of the licensees at the Plough at Eaves suffering any of these punishments: in fact, it was all great fun (see Ale-tasting: the tradition today, pp. 9–10).

The Plough's neighbouring village, Woodplumpton, attracts many visitors, particularly to see the parish church of St Anne. Beside the lych gate are the ancient stocks and in the churchyard is a huge boulder which was said to have been placed over the grave of Meg Shelton, the Fylde witch. She was buried in 1705, but was able to find her way out of her grave – twice! Legend says that the boulder had to be placed on top of her grave to keep her in.

WREA GREEN: *THE GRAPES*

M55 to J3, then A585 towards Kirkham. Bypass Kirkham to Blackpool road. At roundabout cross into Ribby road, B5259. At Wrea Green the pub is on the right.

The village pump stands on the green opposite the Grapes.

Whether you are a cricket player or watcher, a lover of pub lunches or are passionate about English villages, Wrea Green has it all. A summer Sunday, cricket on the Green – the largest in the county and an award winner – the Grapes and the village church beyond: here you have a perfect setting. The cricket club has just celebrated one hundred years on the Green; thirty years ago, or thereabouts, the Boddington family, who once owned the pub, presented a sports changing room at the

The Grapes stands in an unrivalled position facing the green.

The timbered interior heavily decorated with hops.

Grapes. In winter, football followed by chip butties at the Grapes is an old tradition for players and supporters alike.

The Grapes is in an ideal position facing the Green, itself surrounded by beautifully kept cottages and gardens and ancient Cookson's farm. Look for the village pump on the Green and the duck pond, known locally as the 'Dub', because clay daub from it was used for building walls in nearby cottages; licensed fishing is allowed, so it is still a centre of activity.

On sunny days there is competition for the tables outside the front of the Grapes – not surprising, considering the view. Within the pub many changes have taken place, but the traditional atmosphere remains: low ceilings, enormous beams and arches that divide the interior into eight separate dining spaces decorated with hops. Away to the left there is a display of cricket and football photographs; in a case competition trophies are displayed. A passageway past the bar leads to a further extensive area of tables and chairs; Sundays will find them all occupied. Visiting the Grapes on Sundays is a way of life in the Wrea Green district.

The Grapes was once known as the Dumplings, to commemorate the annual apple dumpling competition, with plenty of supplies from the orchards and smallholdings surrounding the Green. One can imagine the excitement. In those days there were no cars, but horses with their packs stabled at the pub and on their way to market goods in Manchester, Liverpool and beyond. Then the railway came – and went; in the days when there was a station here travellers to and from the Fylde coast found that the Grapes was conveniently placed for a pint of refreshment. The fight to bring back the station goes on.

Once again in 2005 the village received the prestigious Lancashire Best Kept Village Award. This is not surprising, as the villagers work hard in teams to maintain high standards of cleanliness, with individual hanging baskets and other floral displays. The competition for best-kept front gardens in various categories is very popular and recognised throughout the north-west of England.

Just opposite the Grapes is the magnificent Millennium Clock; beneath it are sealed capsules from all the local organisations; the contents will be fascinating to researchers one hundred years from now. In spring there will be a full circle of crocuses. The area is still known as the cock fighting pit from years gone by; it is thought that the Earl of Derby had a cock fight here during the Civil War.

There is so much and such a variety of things to see, not least Lancashire's best-kept war memorial. On one beautifully sunny Sunday in September, yet another surprise: opposite the Grapes the area canon was blessing horses (and their riders) that had come to the Green from far and near. The 'best seats in the house' were those occupied by the lucky, or well-informed diners sitting outside the pub, which was, of course, packed out.

A mere 7 miles from the Fylde coast and just an hour's drive from Liverpool, Manchester and Lancaster; even the Lake District, the North Pennines and the Trough of Bowland are within easy reach. Wrea Green should be in everybody's travel plans – and for more than one visit.

ACKNOWLEDGEMENTS

I wish to thank most warmly those people, many of whom are now friends, whose contributions made this book possible. It was more than the provision of information, valuable as that was: their shared interest and enthusiasm to see on record much that had never been written down made the research work doubly satisfying. Generous loans of old documents and illustrations were freely offered and opportunities to take photographs granted without hesitation.

Whenever background information was needed or guidance sought, the following Lancashire organisations were unfailingly helpful: County Library Service; County Museum Service; County Developments Ltd; tourist information centres; Pendle Heritage Centre, Barrowford; Touchstones Rochdale; Saddleworth Museum & Art Gallery. Help was equally appreciated from CAMRA branches and the Britannia Coconut Dancers. Outside the county the following were most helpful: Henley-in-Arden Branch Library and Henley Court Leet; Samuel Smith, the Old Brewery, Tadcaster.

Individuals whose help is gratefully acknowledged are: Simon Entwistle (Clitheroe); Alan Greening (Wrea Green); Matt Jackson (Lancaster); Alan Robson (Henley-in-Arden Photography); Steve Strickland (Roughlee) and Sylvia Wood (Stalybridge Station Buffet); also the licensees of the following pubs: Redwell Inn, Arkholme; Old Man & Scythe, Bolton; Stork, Conder Green; Royal Oak, Garstang; Victoria, Great Harwood; White Bull, Ribchester; Plough at Eaves, Woodplumpton.

Any errors or omissions in the book are entirely my responsibility. To anyone who gave help in any way and is not mentioned above I offer my grateful thanks and most sincere apologies.